I0808124

When a Factory Becomes a Home

Adaptive Reuse for Living

Imprint

The Deutsche Nationalbibliothek lists this publication in the Deutsche Nationalbibliografie; detailed bibliographic data are available on the Internet at http://dnb.dnb.de

ISBN 978-3-03768-240-1
© 2019 by Braun Publishing AG
www.braun-publishing.ch

The work is copyright protected. Any use outside of the close boundaries of the copyright law, which has not been granted permission by the publisher, is unauthorized and liable for prosecution. This especially applies to duplications, translations, microfilming, and any saving or processing in electronic systems.

1st edition 2019

Editor: Editorial Office van Uffelen
Editorial staff and layout: Julia Heinemann, Linda Prey, Lisa Rogers
Basic graphic concept: Michaela Prinz, Berlin
Cover and revised graphic design: STUDIO LZ, Stuttgart
Reproduction: Bild1Druck GmbH, Berlin

All of the information in this volume has been compiled to the best of the editor's knowledge. It is based on the information provided to the publisher by the architects' and designers' offices and excludes any liability. The publisher assumes no responsibility for its accuracy or completeness as well as copyright discrepancies and refers to the specified sources (architects' and designers' offices). All rights to the photographs are property of the photographer (please refer to the picture credits).

When a Factory Becomes a Home

Chris van Uffelen

Adaptive Reuse for Living

BRAUN

Contents

The best is yet to come …

Reuse, changes made to the preexisting structure to transform it into a new type of building is an everyday phenomenon. If a building survives longer than it is needed to serve its initial purpose, it can either be demolished or transformed into something new. And what can be done with an imposing antique Roman city gate in Trier? Let's turn it into a chapel (Porta Nigra)! Or even a medieval defense tower in Paris? It was first a castle, then a palace and finally the world's largest museum (Louvre). And what was to become of all those monasteries and palaces after the French Revolution? Why not transform them into universities, barracks and clinics, of course! And what to do with the Jeu de Paume when this kind of indoor tennis went out of fashion? Sport halls can be converted to ballrooms, churches, libraries, or even museums – like the famous Galerie Nationale du Jeu de Paume next to the Place de la Concorde in Paris. And how might one reuse the gigantic mass of an amphitheater? Well, they can either be used as a handy stone quarry (Colosseum in Rome), or extended to serve as residential buildings, as is the case in Florence and Lucca. In Lucca it is still possible to make out the edge of the original site of the ancient amphitheater, while in Florence, it is only when one looks at street maps of the city and aerial views that it becomes apparent that the route between the Piazza della Signoria and the Piazza di Santa Croce on the Via De' Bentaccordi was once the site of gladiator fights. It is impossible to see this if you don't know what was once there. It now looks like an ordinary city quarter with residential buildings, but large parts of the original structure do still exist inside the dwellings. The fact that parts of the foundations and original walls were preserved was largely due to economic reasons. And economic feasibility remains an important point in favor of reuse projects.

However, today the environmental considerations carry even more weight. While on the one hand reuse projects require less energy as the buildings on the site are neither demolished nor build from scratch, they nevertheless often do poorly in terms of energy consumption when compared to their highly-insulated modern counterparts. Approximately 70 percent of the energy used during a building's lifetime comes from lighting, heating or cooling, while the other 30 percent is used for its initial construction. This so called "embodied energy" – mining and processing of natural resources to manufacturing, transport and product delivery of parts as well as of the complete building – might outreach the energy saved by modern techniques and good insulation of old walls may be more environmentally friendly.

The transformation of a building into a residential space might not always be the most obvious use, but it is one for which there is great need. After all, it is rather unlikely that a site that once housed a shipyard (Amsterdam, Max van Aerschot, 2007) or a trade fair complex (Cologne, HPP Architekten, 2009) would be abandoned at exactly the moment when there is need for an empty structure to be reused, for a television studio, for example. But residential properties can be built pretty much anywhere, even in former schools, factories, garages or churches, warehouses, silos or bunkers. In rural settings, it is usually agricultural buildings that are transformed into residential properties; in cities it is former office buildings and factories that dominate the reuse trend. The companies occupying such buildings are increasingly moving to premises on the outskirts of the cities, thus leaving behind large empty buildings. Most of these share the common characteristic that the building depth is often too large to easily accommodate the relatively small rooms required for residential purposes, thus architects are faced with the challenge of providing light and ventilation. Religious buildings are increasingly being used for residential purposes. These are officially secularized and often given an artistic purpose initially, in order to ensure a certain distance between the former religious use and the intended residential purpose. This clear division of functions is not necessary for most secular buildings, but it is nevertheless sometimes desired. The most famous example of this is the wrapping of the Reichstag in Berlin by Christo and Jeanne-Claude (1995) before Norman Foster transformed it into the "Bundestag im Reichstag" building (1999).

Similar to Norman Foster's transformation of the Reichstag building, many residential reuse projects emphasize the contrast between the preexisting and the new building substance, instead of attempting to conceal this with fake historical additions. The original building with its traces of history has been preserved and only minimal interventions have been carried out. In the case of this preservation project, the reconstructed sections are plain to see, with the layers marking the passage of time. The old and the new are easy to differentiate esthetically, with the new not attempting to fuse with the old. It is this contrast between two or more real forms of expression, typical of their era, that bring a building to life and give it charm. This is an exciting way of making the past part of both the present and the future.

Above Coop Himmelb(l)au: Gasometer B with 254 apartments, Vienna, Austria, 2001 **Center** The former second-century amphitheater of Lucca, Piazza dell'Anfiteatro, Italy **Below** Riccardo Bofil: Cement factory residence, Sant Just Desvern, Spain, 1973

1885 → 2013

In the project Tribeca Loft a Civil War-era warehouse has been transformed into a residence.

In Manhattan's Tribeca North area, the top floor of a Civil War-era warehouse has been transformed into a warm and welcoming residence. The main focuses of the architectural intervention were the relocation of an existing mezzanine and the addition of a glass-enclosed planted courtyard. A retractable glass roof over the courtyard connects to the new roof garden above and brings views and daylight into what was once a dark loft. Embracing the building's industrial past, much of the structural character of the romanesque revival building has been preserved or exposed. The design engages in a visual discourse between new and old, juxtaposing the heavy timbers and masonry with modern insertions of smooth, reflective surfaces and new built-in cabinetry using reclaimed and local materials. A walnut fascia unifies this multilevel residence. The new green roof terrace, which utilizes reclaimed bluestone pavers and native plant species, insulates the spaces below.

Architect Andrew Franz Architect **Completion** 2013 **Original building** Warehouse / manufacturing, 1884–85 **Gross floor area** 280 m² **Number of rooms** 4 **Number of residents** 2 **Address** New York, NY, USA

Arched windows and brick walls hint at the building's industrial past, while additional glazing provide enough daylight.

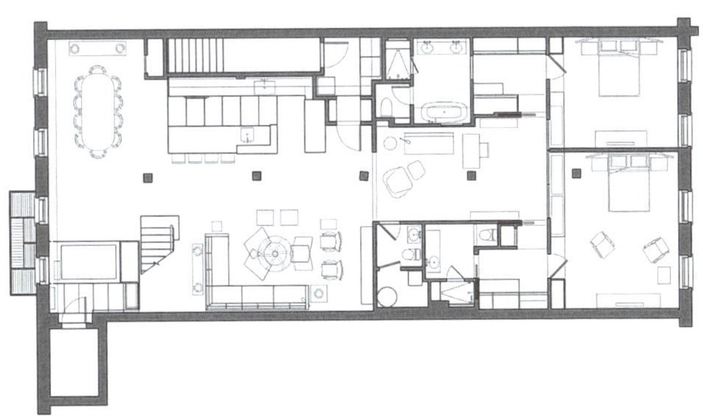

Ground floor plan

1912 → 2017

The former school house now houses new apartments.

The architects have transformed this early 20th-century school building into six apartments. The starting point for the design was to make optimal use of the monumental space, the tall windows and original details. The wall between two classrooms has been removed to create a large loft-like living space. The ceiling height of five meters offered possibilities for creating new intermediate floors and more intimate areas. In addition to the characteristic windows between the classrooms and corridors, a few strategically placed new openings create new lines of sight and increase the sense of spatiality and light. In the hallway, the original yellow glazed brickwork has been preserved. The kitchen, situated in the high part of the living space, is organized around a large concrete island. The five original school toilets have been given new functions and a mirror across the rear wall of the bathroom accentuates the length of the school hallway.

Architect eklund_terbeek architects **Completion** 2017 **Original building** School, 1912 **Gross floor area before** 140 m² **Gross floor area after** 200 m² **Number of rooms before** 3 **Number of rooms after** 6 **Number of apartments** 6 **Number of residents** 3 **Address** Duyststraat 28, 3023 EE Rotterdam, the Netherlands

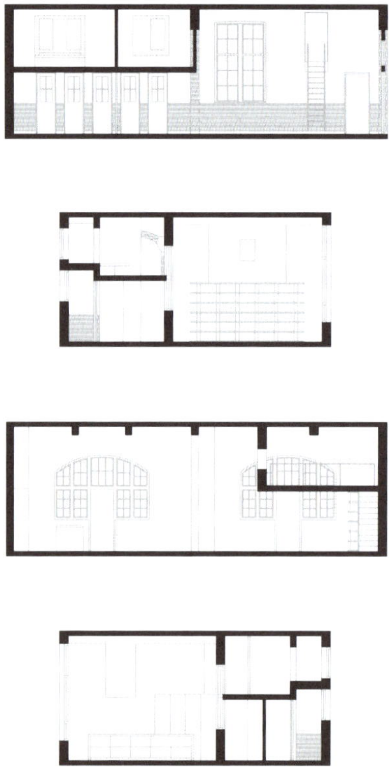

Sections

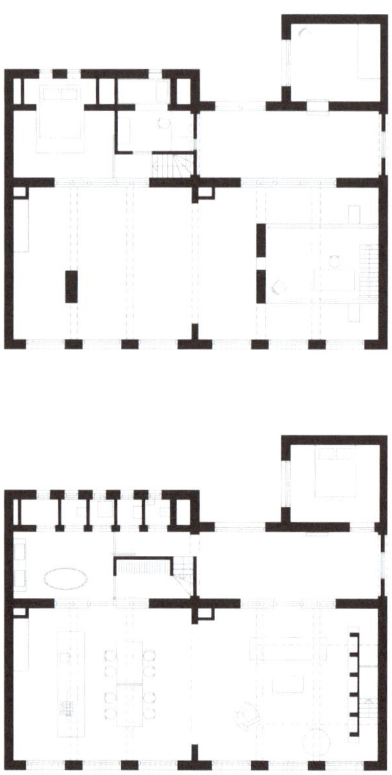

Floor plans

The contrasts between high and low, open and closed, original details and contemporary additions highlight the experience of space.

19th century → 2015

Larch Barn combines modern living with Alpine history.

This project involved the transformation of an old barn into a primary residence for the clients. New volumes have been inserted at the back of the property, ensuring a minimum impact on the main façades. On the ground floor, the new volume has been embedded into the ground and accommodates a garage, bathroom, entrance and equipment room. The visible part of the extension on the first floor breaks away from the old barn with its contemporary cladding and roof overhang detail. The openings were sized accurately to frame specific views of the valley but also to respect the original building. The built-in furnishings were planned down to the finest detail in order to use every single space available. Solar panels, photovoltaic panels and a double flow ventilation were integrated into the construction. Special consideration was given to the quality of the construction materials, making it the first building of its type to be certified with the Minergie P label in Switzerland.

16

Architect Alp'Architecture Sàrl **Completion** 2015 **Original building** Barn, 19th century **Gross floor area before** 50 m² **Gross floor area after** 150 m² **Number of rooms** 2 **Number of apartments** 1 **Number of residents** 2 **Address** Le Rosay, 1948 Lourtier, Switzerland

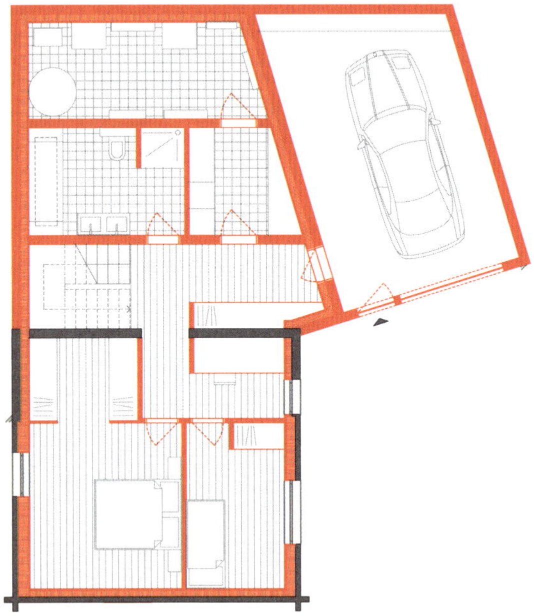

Ground floor plan

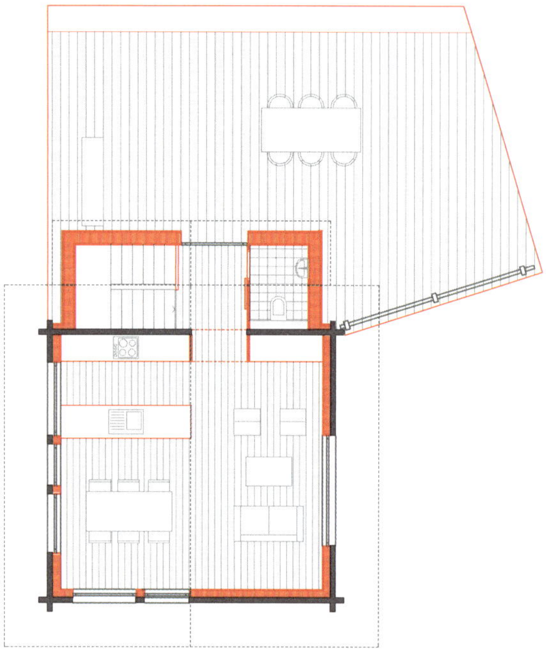

First floor plan

Reusing the original planks helped to create an authentic design.

1880 → 2015

Chapel on the Hill, a former Methodist church, now serves as a comfortable home.

Set in the very best walking area of the beautiful North Pennines, this stunning chapel conversion with its historic building fabric and modern interior design is a real Teesdale landmark. The original windows of the 19th century building have been reopened, framing dramatic views. As the existing building was in a poor state of disrepair and had been vacant for many years, the aim of the reconstruction project was to bring this unique property back to life. Installing services and sewage treatment was one of the very first tasks. Once a new level had been installed, all new bespoke timber frame windows and shutters were installed to complement the unique style and details of the chapel. The kitchen takes advantage of the Gothic windows and the beautiful views of the surrounding landscape. Modern, stylish and yet in the context of the location and its history the interior design complements the ensemble.

Architect Evolution Design **Completion** 2015 **Original building** Methodist chapel, 1880 **Gross floor area after** 141 m^2 **Number of rooms** 4 **Number of apartments** 1 **Number of residents** Up to 7 **Address** Forest-in-Teesdale, County Durham, UK

Taking advantage of the Gothic style, this ensemble combines luxury and history.

Ground floor plan

1930 → 2015

Now known as Penthouse V, this former movie theater offers a spacious living environment with a clear and comfortable atmosphere.

Architect destilat **Completion** 2015 **Original building** Cinema by Franz Baumgartner, 1930 **Gross floor area** 250 m² **Number of rooms before** 3 **Number of rooms after** 4 **Number of apartments** 4 **Number of residents** 7 **Address** Pörtschach, Austria

Due to the height of the pre-existing structure, this apartment is characterized by an airy atmosphere.

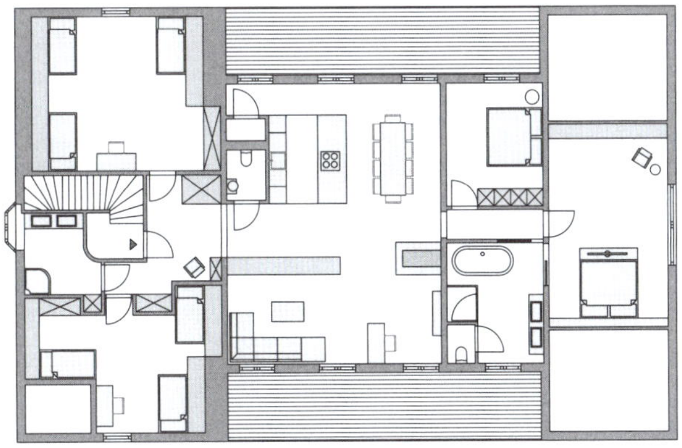

Ground floor plan

During the revitalization of the former Werner movie theater in Pörtschach, part of the roof structure was raised to make space for a large loft conversion. The new apartment features a large living room with a so-called camouflage kitchen, also designed by destilat. The fronts of the kitchen units have been fitted with cement fiber panels. These have been arranged at angles, introducing a fresh design element and a welcome counterpoint to the relaxed atmosphere of the living room. When choosing the materials and fixtures and fittings, particular attention was paid to their practical implementation and user-friendly aspects. Inspired by textures, this approach and the use of materials such as milled cement fiber façade panels for the unit fronts subtly reference Austrian post-war architecture.

1984 → 2016

The former Philips Lighting office complex now houses 665 comfortable apartments.

The former Philips Lighting head office now houses more than 665 lofts and apartments. The building's structure and the concrete staircases have been preserved, but the façades has been given new vertically sliding lower fronts. The residents of the 616 apartments are mostly singles and expats. A completely new layer with 49 penthouses and spacious terraces has been built on the roof, from where one can enjoy a magnificent view of the city. The ceiling height of the lofts is a spacious four meters and the fully open façades allow plenty of natural light to enter. But even in the small apartments, this project contains all that is necessary to make small-scale housing comfortable. The coffee bar on the ground floor eliminates the need for an espresso machine and a desk in the apartment. The design of the sliding fronts was inspired by the windows of cruise ships.

Architect diederendirrix **Completion** 2016 **Original building** Offices and laboratories, 1973–1984 **Gross floor area** 43,000 m^2 **Number of apartments** 665 **Address** Victoriapark, 5611 BM, Eindhoven, the Netherlands

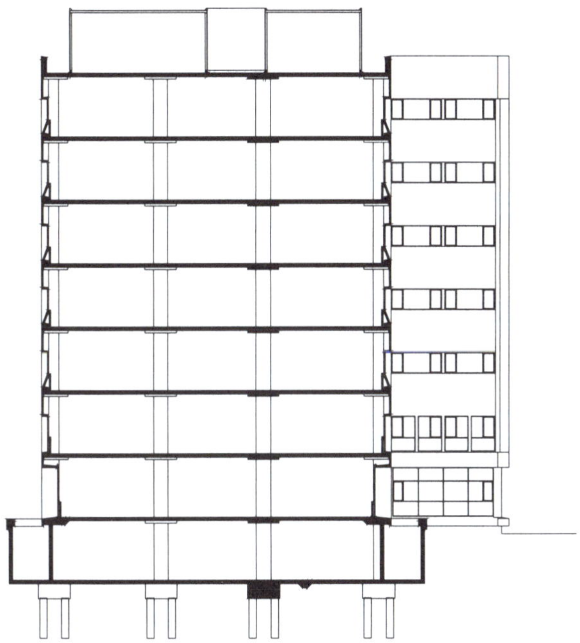

Lighting house section before transformation

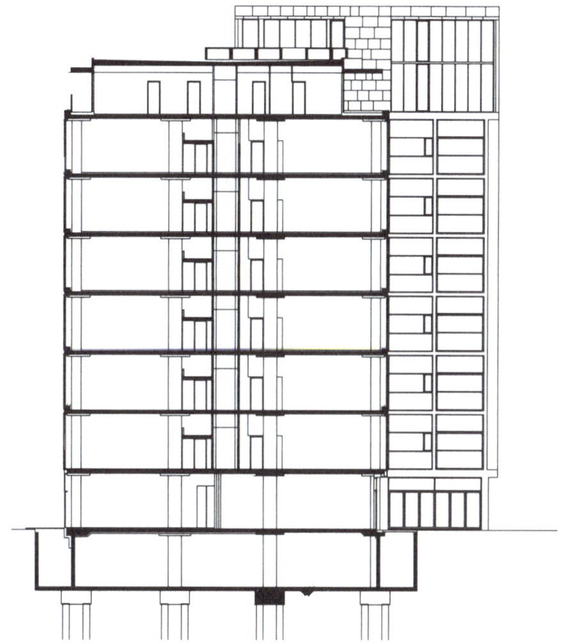

Lighting house section after transformation

Offering all the amenities of a modern lifestyle, these former offices have become the perfect living environment for singles and expats.

1810 → 2016

The transformation of the Little House in the Campo created a contemporary residence that appears as traditional as its predecessor in terms of its architectural style.

On a mountain in the rugged northern part of Ibiza lies this beautiful "finca". What formerly served as stables and storage, has now been transformed into a contemporary house. Basic materials have been used to maintain the character of the original building. The authentic Sabina beams have been preserved, just like the original ancient stone walls in the kitchen and bathroom. The architects used only materials that are traditionally used on the island, such as the Iroko window frames, concrete and stone walls plastered with white chalk. Only the walls and parts of the roof could be preserved. Electricity, water and sewage systems were entirely absent. Contrasting aspects like old and new, sleek and rustic, light and dark determine the design. Water comes from a private well and solar panels have been installed to provide hot water, floor heating and electricity. The cottage operates completely off-grid and is self-sustainable.

EEN EIGEN EILAND

Architect Standard Studio **Furniture** Modern Vintage **Completion** 2016 **Original building** Farm, 1810 **Gross floor area** 45 m² **Number of rooms before** 1 **Number of rooms after** 3 **Number of apartments** 1 **Number of residents** 2 **Address** Ibiza Campo, Spain

Using traditional materials has ensured that the architectural style has been preserved.

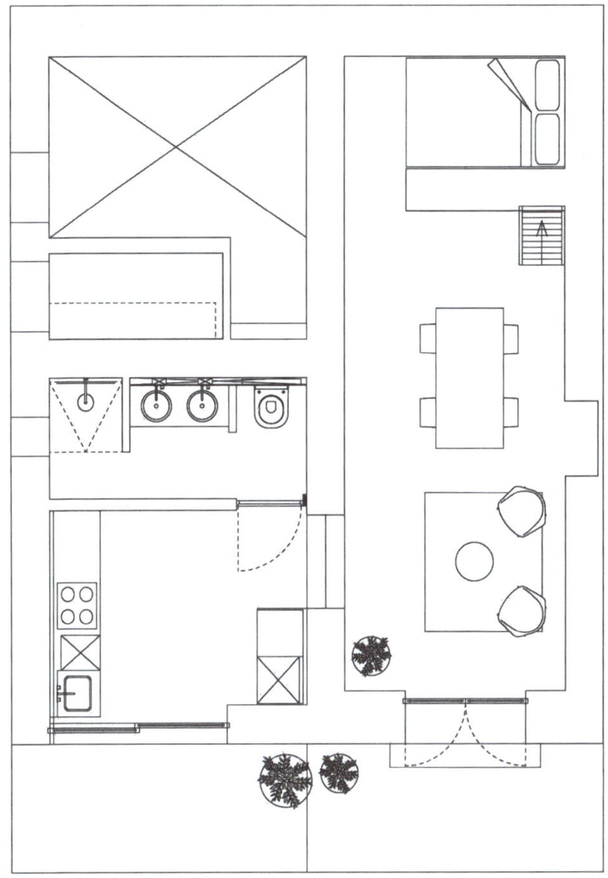

Ground floor plan

19th century → 2016

Javornice Distillery breathes new life into the 19th century farm building.

Located in the Bohemian village of Javornice, a new, partially reconstructed area now stands on the site of a farmhouse from the late 19th century. This new building is located beside a small fruit distillery and other buildings. The reconstruction work has altered the original layout and location of buildings, which were in very poor condition. This resulted in the demolition of all modern outbuildings, including roofs and trusses. Only the basic materials and some main supporting walls were preserved. Then a new residence was built in the attic, and the old barn was replaced by a wooden house with a garage. The architects' aim was to preserve most of the original architectural features and where this was not possible they replaced them with similar characteristic details transferred from other buildings in South Bohemia. For the new buildings, new materials were selected that are contemporary, but also respect the original structure.

Architect ADR **Completion** 2016 **Original building** Farmhouse, 19th century **Gross floor area before** 319.5 m^2 **Gross floor area after** 483.5 m^2 **Number of rooms before** 12 **Number of rooms after** 25 **Number of apartments** 4 **Number of residents** 12 **Address** Javornice, U Dubu, Czech Republic

Adapting the original Bohemian structures where possible, led to a concept that respects the traditional character of the former buildings.

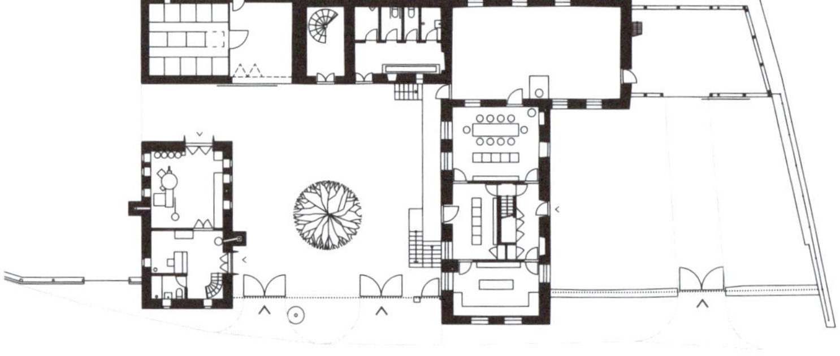

Ground floor plan

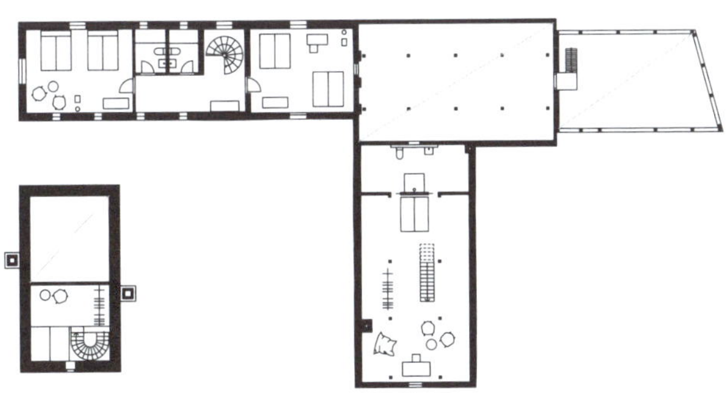

First floor plan

Architect asdfg Architekten, Loeper Schmitz Grenz **Completion** 2015 **Original building** Miller's house, approx. 1844, reuse as office complex **Gross floor area** 400 m² **Number of rooms before** Approx. 15 **Number of rooms after** Approx. 7 **Number of apartments** 1 **Number of residents** 5 **Address** Metzerstrasse 13a, 10405 Berlin, Germany

1844 → 2015

Once a miller's house, the Müller-Haus am Prenzlauer Berg later served as an office complex, before being transformed into this stunning residence.

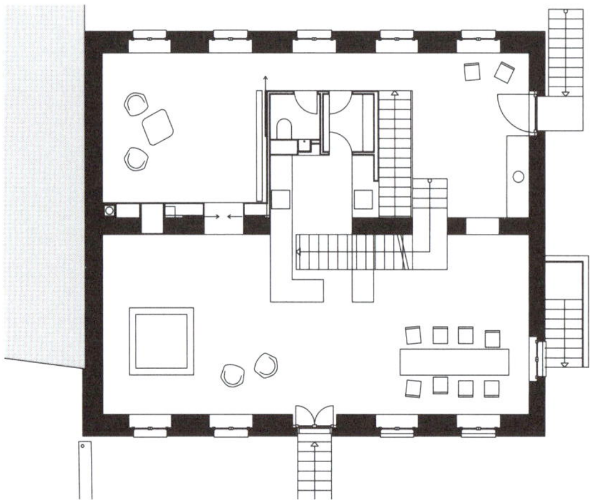

Ground floor plan

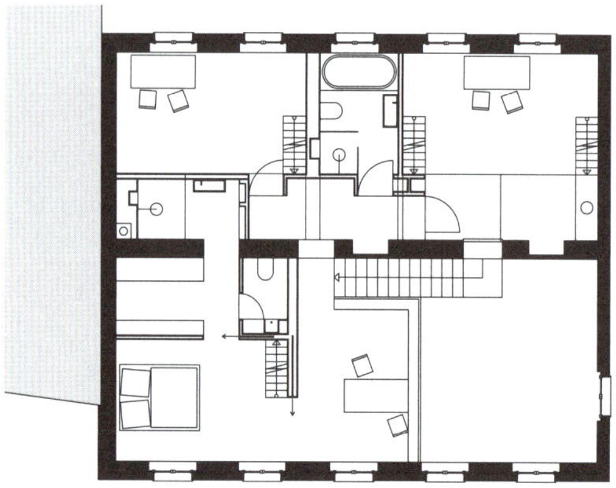

First floor plan

The façade structure emphasizes the historical character of the building, while the small rooms have been opened up to create a sense of spaciousness.

This project involved the renovation of Prenzlauer Berg's oldest house, turning it into an elegant, modern residence. Both the history of the property and the location presented a challenge. For example, the local building authority insisted that the façade be reconstructed based on one of the original sketches. But because there were no remaining traces of the original façade, the lines of the elevation sketch have been reinterpreted as differences in height. In the 2-D sketch, the new façade looks exactly the same as the historical sketch. Depending on how the light falls, the façade creates a dynamic play of light and shadow. The small spaces inside have been opened out to create large open rooms. The exposed brick walls inside are visible throughout the entire width of the house and support the dialogue that has been established between the past and the present.

1916 → 2009

The extra-ordinary Lofts in Barcelona are located in a former sugar factory.

This project transforms 200 hectares of industrial land in the Poblenou district into an innovative area offering modern spaces for the strategic concentration of intensive knowledge-based activities. This initiative is also an urban refurbishment project and a new model for cities responding to challenges posed by the knowledge-based society. In this historical sugar factory, a clear focus has been placed on obtaining a finished product that is both high-quality and unique. The project was inspired by the appearance and character of the original industrial space. The former sugar factory warehouses have been sliced vertically following the rhythm of the roof trusses, converting each segment in two and three-story lofts. The existing buildings of various levels have been transformed into large, open-space single-level units.

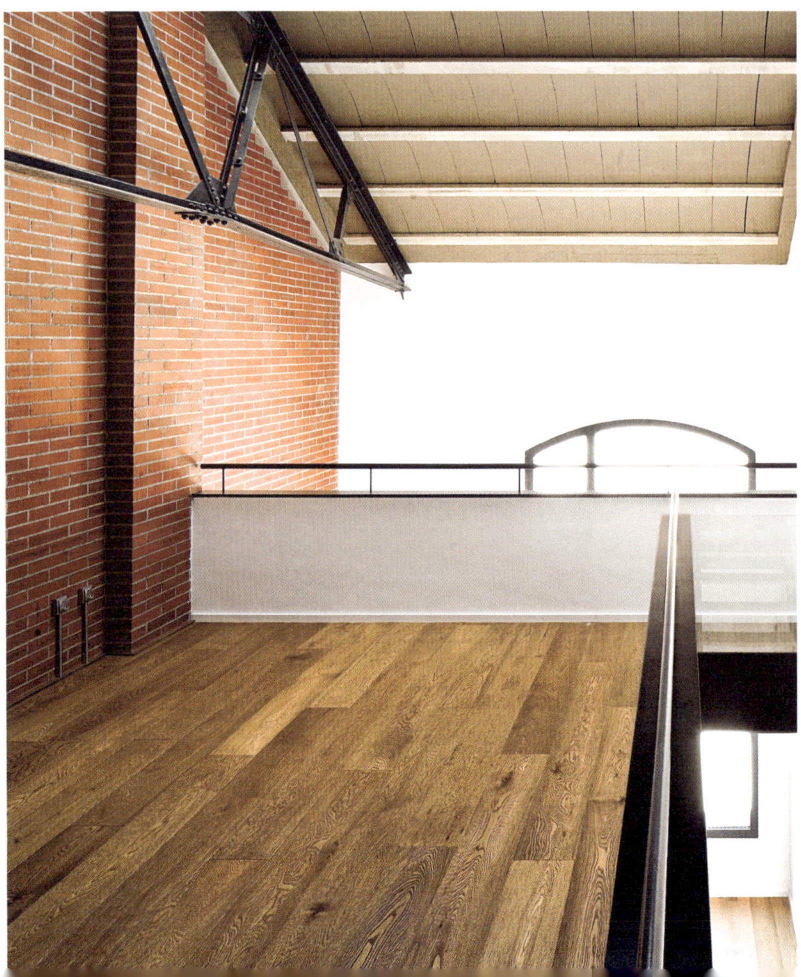

Architect Garcés – de Seta – Bonet Architects with Berta Rovira architect **Completion** 2009 **Original building** Sugar factory, 1916 **Gross floor area** 7,969 m² **Number of rooms before** 4 **Number of rooms after** 30 **Number of apartments** 30 **Number of residents** 90 **Address** Passatge de Mas de Roda, Barcelona, Spain

A distinctive ensemble has been created by matching the preexisting industrial design with high-quality elements.

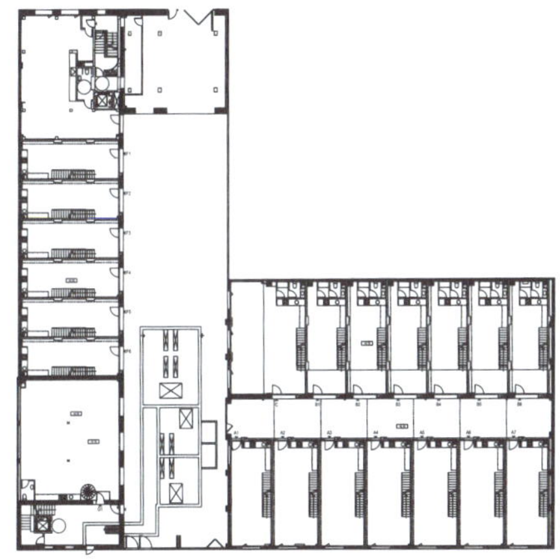

Ground floor plan

1880 → 2013

For Manor House Stables, former stable blocks have been transformed into a cozy family home.

These historical stables in the Hampshire countryside have been transformed into a contemporary family home. The history and character of the stables was very much a driving force in the design. The existing exposed timber interior walls have been cleaned, stripped back and refurbished to reveal an exquisite amount of craftsmanship. To retain the property's character, a clean, contemporary and neutral approach was taken to the rest of the renovation. The original horse troughs have been cleaned and converted for use as sinks, while the old horse ties act as towel rings in the bathrooms and some original doors have also been preserved. The stable building now accommodates three large double bedrooms, with two bathrooms. The building is a long single-story property with long continuous views and the layout has been divided between sleeping and living areas. The open-plan kitchen with dining area is located at the heart of the home, leading into the lounge. New windows and roof lights fitted throughout give the entire home a warm, bright and clean feel; creating an excellent environment as a backdrop for family life.

Bright, warm rooms have been created that nevertheless preserve the history of the original stable building.

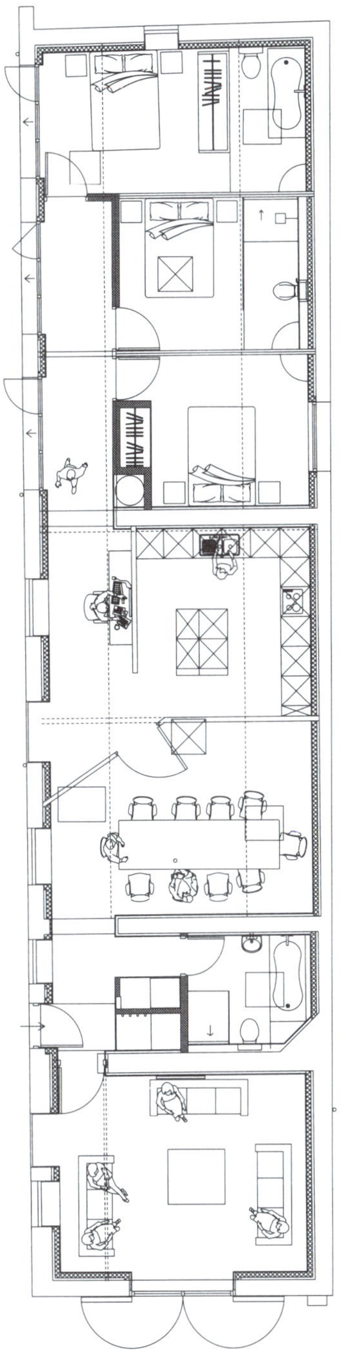

Ground floor plan

Architect AR Design Studio **Completion** 2013 **Original building** Stable block, 1880 **Gross floor area before** 136 m² **Gross floor area after** 125 m² **Number of rooms** 7 **Number of apartments** 1 **Address** Winchester, UK

1920 → 2013

This project implemented the repurposing of a garage into a loft-like house.

This project involved the creation of two apartments in a former automobile garage in a rural setting. The design aimed to maintain the industrial character of the pre-existing building. The lengthy planning process envisaged the demolition of the garage building, which shadowed the main construction, reconstruction work on the roof to give it a steeper tilt, and the inclusion of a larger skylight. The windows were replaced, although they maintained their position, with some being extended down to the floor. On the ground floor, large aluminum frames have been used as these have the desired industrial character. The ground floor is now a large loft with a 100-square-meter living area and centrally organized living room fire, the construction of which also supports the ceiling. A sculptural steel staircase leads to the upper floor where three bedrooms, a large atelier and two bathrooms are located.

Architect Planungsbüro Schilling **Completion** 2013 **Original building** Garage, approx. 1920 **Gross floor area before** 150 m² **Gross floor area after** 252 m² **Number of rooms before** 2 **Number of rooms after** 6 **Number of apartments** 1 **Number of residents** 4 **Address** Parsdorf, Munich, Germany

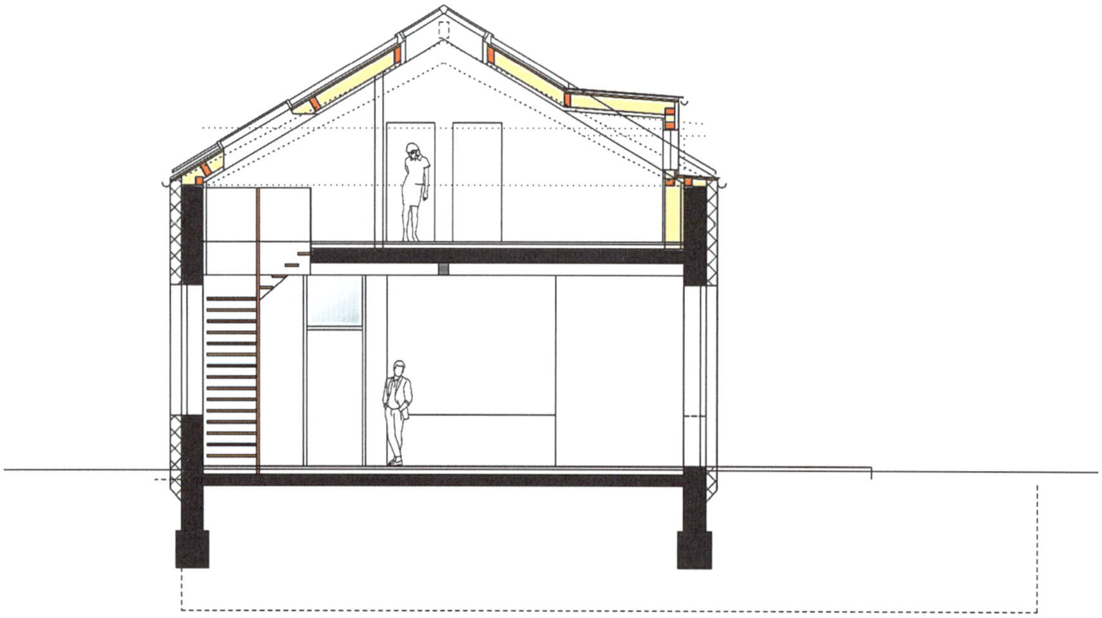

Section

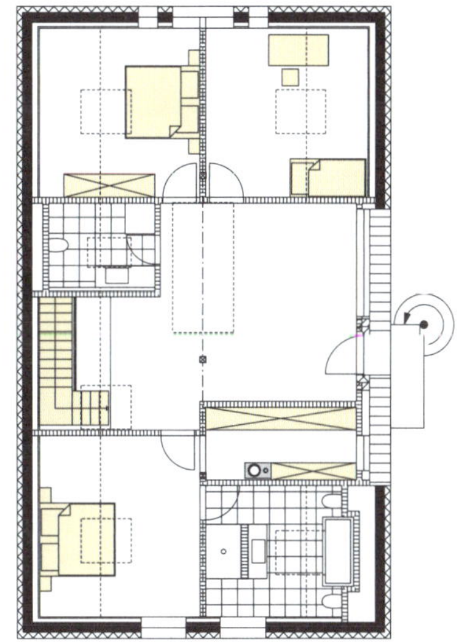

First floor plan

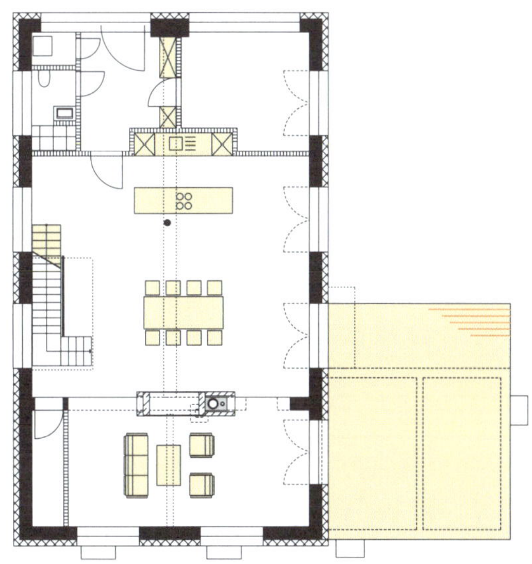

Ground floor plan

Some details recall the former building and the garage's unique history.

Unknown → 2014

The Office Complex Transformation demonstrates the metamorphosis of a former demure building into a trendy lifestyle ensemble.

In order to transform this former office complex into attractive apartments, it was necessary to give the narrow and sober corridors a complete makeover. The design establishes a colorful band that stretches over the floors, walls and ceilings. The colors range from pink, orange and red, to blue and white stripes, warm gold and deep red. A change of color on the floor subtly simulates daylight. The unique wall designs are inspired by the stories of famous fashion designers, thus forging a connection to the fashion context of this apartment building in Dusseldorf. The design pays homage to prominent fashion designers such as Issey Miyake and Vivienne Westwood. The use of modular systems improved the economic feasibility of the design.

Architect 100% interior Sylvia Leydecker **Completion** 2014 **Original building** Office building **Address** Dusseldorf, Germany

Floor sections

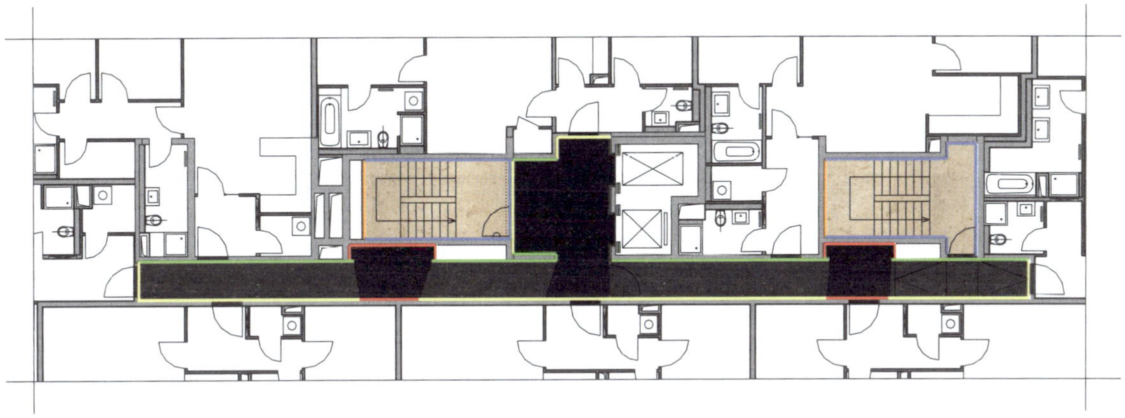

Ground floor plan

By creating individual wall designs, a vivid framework has been established, suitable for contemporary living concepts in an environment dedicated to fashion and design.

1900 → 2016

House Moser – transforming a barn into a modern living space.

This approximately 150-year-old hay barn has been dismantled and then reconstructed on its original site as a cozy retreat. The building has been built on a new concrete foundation and the new structure comprises two wall sections, a suspended ceiling with a wooden beam construction and a solid roof section constructed of plywood boards with roof insulation. The rest of the space is enclosed by triple-glazed "fixglass" with just a few doors and windows. The spatial program takes into consideration the original layout and use of materials. Seen from the outside, the building remains largely unaltered; but the architectural intervention protects it from decaying or being torn down.

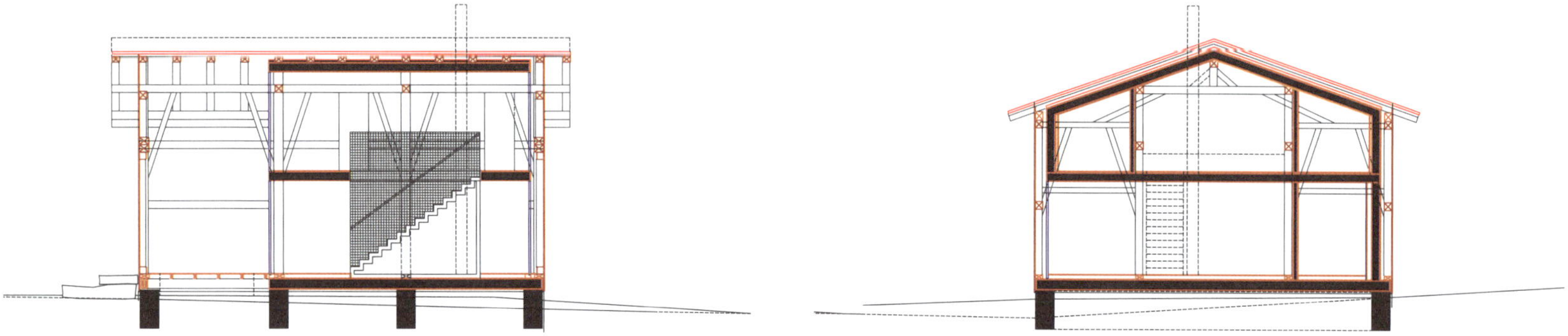

Sections

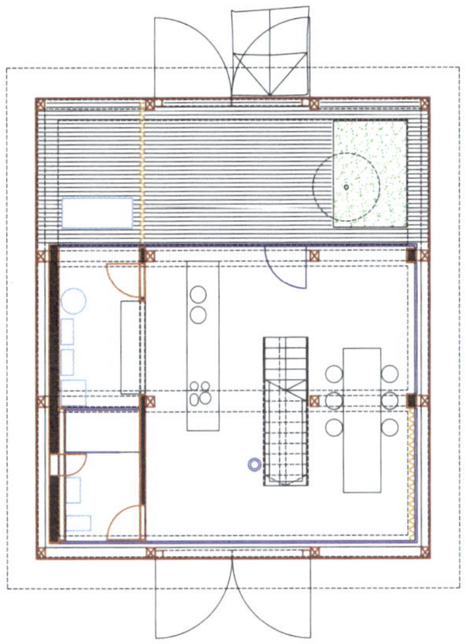

Ground floor plan

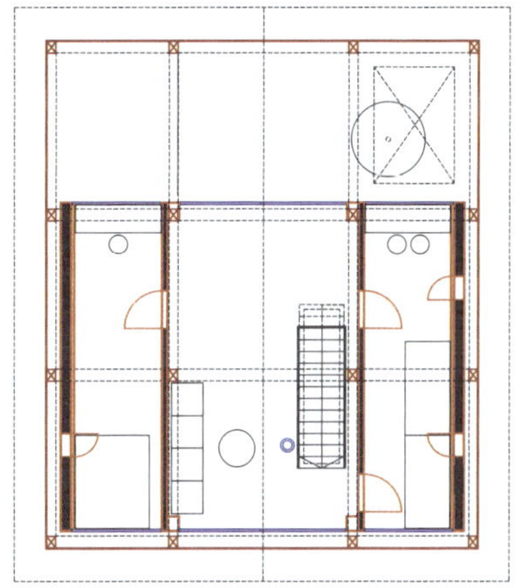

First floor plan

Architect madritsch*pfurtscheller **Completion** 2016 **Original building** Barn, approx. 1900 **Gross floor area** 105 m² **Number of rooms before** 1 **Number of rooms after** 6 **Number of apartments** 1 **Number of residents** 6 **Address** Stackler 57, 6167 Neustift, Austria

The reconstruction of this barn references the building's history.

This project breathes new life into a former bunker. Surrounded by middle-class residences and a railway station belonging to Hamburg Altona, this listed building has been transformed into an extravagant second base for Kramer & Co. The most challenging aspects of the project were adhering to the strict historical building preservation guidelines, and solving the problems posed by the unusual characteristics of the existing structure. Openings for the windows and doors had to be cut out of the solid walls. Characteristic aspects, such as the wooden elements in the stairwell or the generator in the cellar have been maintained and restored – despite their dilapidated condition. Even though these no longer serve their original function, they nevertheless emphasize the original importance of the bunker and preserve an important part of history.

1939 → 2016

Now an extraordinary residential space, this former bunker in Hamburg houses a contemporary apartment.

Architect Kramer & Co **Completion** 2016 **Original building** Bunker, 1939 **Gross floor area after** 120 m² **Number of rooms** 1 **Number of apartments** 1 **Number of residents** 2 **Address** Bülowstrasse, Hamburg, Germany

An elegant interior design melts with the rough bunker structures to create a unique living environment.

1800 → 2016

Once a Slovenian barn, Vrhe House now offers all the comforts of a modern living environment.

This former barn building is reminiscent of a hayrack structure, the traditional structure has been maintained but given a new and modern flair. The architects paid careful attention to detail, using oak pegs and structural details in keeping with the original architecture. The framework of the barn remains largely untouched, preserving its expressive elements. The new house is essentially a skillful and hidden modern architectural implant of a "pavilion in a hayrack". The design seeks to maintain a certain harmony that exists between the original structure and its surroundings. From the outside, the building respectfully handles all the essential aspects of the vernacular Slovenian country architecture, while the interior displays a modern living environment.

Architect Styria Arhitektura **Landscape design** Aleš Koprivšek **Completion** 2016 **Original building** Barn, approx. 1800 **Gross floor area** 479 m² **Number of rooms** 3 **Number of apartments** 1 **Number of residents** 2 **Address** Vrhe, Slovenia

A hidden modern pavilion creates a new ensemble that maintains a strong relationship to the surrounding countryside.

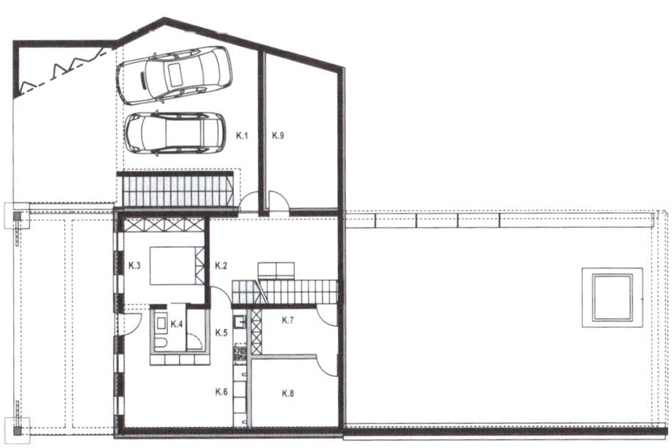

Ground floor plan

This former chocolate factory, built around 1870, was renowned for being the home of a number of rather wild communities at the end of the seventies. Most of the factory floors are in private hands now and this is also the case for Apartment H, even though it was and will be still used as a shared flat by the daughter of the clients and her friends. Mandatory fire prevention measures on the original cast iron bearing structure made it necessary to completely remove all non-structural additions from the apartment. This opportunity was used to overhaul and renovate the whole apartment, making it ready for the next decades in one big step. The new floor plan now provides the perfect layout for the needs of the flatmates. A generous open-plan kitchen and living room, three rooms of the same size, a big bathroom with a shower and an extra toilet for guests and the morning rush. A beautiful place not only as a shared apartment but also as a future retreat for the clients themselves.

1870 → 2015

Once part of a chocolate factory, Apartment H has been transformed into an extra-ordinary home in one of Berlin's most vibrant areas.

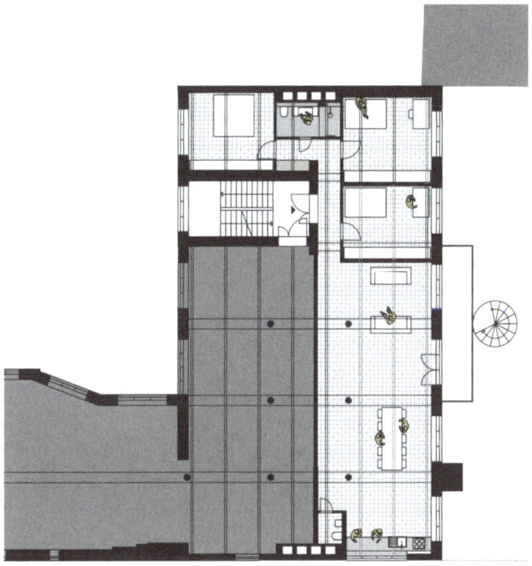

Ground floor plan after transformation

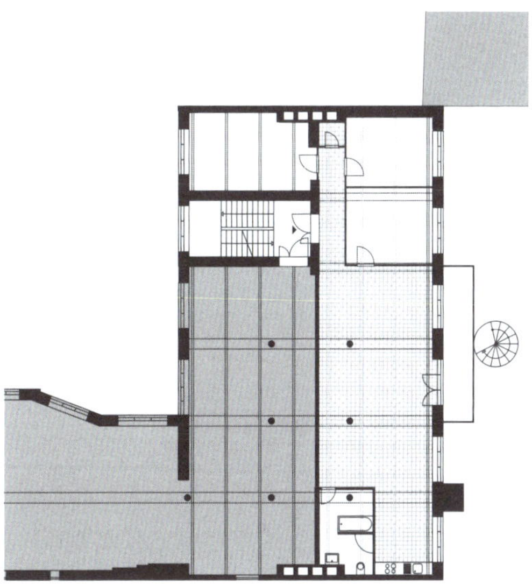

Ground floor plan before transformation

Architect IFUB* - Institut für u. Baukunst **Completion** 2015 **Original building** Chocolate factory, 1870 **Gross floor area** 187 m² **Number of rooms** 4 **Number of apartments** 1 **Number of residents** 1 **Address** Neukölln, 12047 Berlin, Germany

Open-plan structures determine the new design which is highlighted by the preserved industrial elements.

1924 → 2014

This project involved the conversion of St. Luke's Chapel into apartment complexes.

Architect Morscher Architekten **Completion** 2014 **Original building** Chapel, 1924 **Gross floor area before** 440 m² **Gross floor area after** 560 m² **Number of rooms before** 7 **Number of rooms after** 16 **Number of apartments** 3 **Address** Balmweg 5, 3007 Berne, Switzerland

This project is located in a neighborhood in the Swiss city of Berne and involved the transformation of a former chapel from 1924. Two new apartments have been built in the double-story nave, in addition to a preexisting flat in the attic. A floor-to-ceiling concrete beam on the upper floor spans across the full length of the nave and serves as a sustaining partition wall between the new apartments. This construction ensured that the typical church windows could be retained. The frames of the windows have been preserved, with new triple glazing on the outside. The south façade has been completely rebuilt and opened up with generous sliding doors and projecting balconies that look out over the garden and the neighborhood beyond. Historical features on the outside were maintained wherever possible. Inside, the design is characterized by a minimalist material pallet.

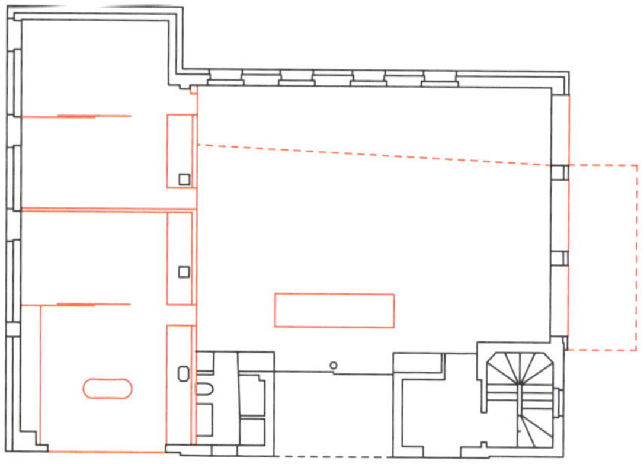

Ground floor plan

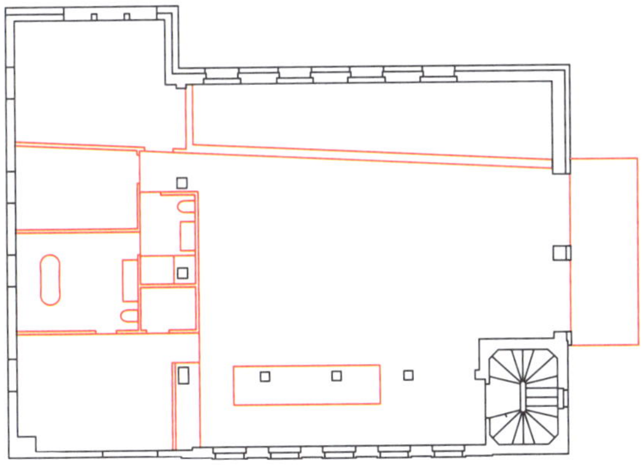

First floor plan

Arched windows and open spaces recall the former religious function.

1890 → 2010

The building called Flag breathes new life into an old farmhouse in Austria.

This small building gives a confident and self-contained impression. The various components are grouped around a small courtyard in the traditional fashion. The design is characterized by the appropriate yet confident interaction with preexisting structures and the addition of modern concepts of use in the existing context and energetic adaptation of the former building. The extension building adds just under 60 square meters of additional living area. The new building follows the boundary of the plot and continues the roof geometry of the other buildings. The north side is supported by V supports and juts out over the access route, providing a covered area. The building shell comprises prefabricated panels and opens out towards the south and the east with large windows. The concrete floor and wood-clad roof accompany the open kitchen workbench. The fleece panels on the north side aid noise protection and function as a backrest for the bench. The large windows ensure passive warming and a reduction of heating costs.

ANIMALS

Architect propeller z **Completion** 2010 **Original building** Yard, 1890 **Gross floor area** 65–120 m² **Number of rooms before** 4 **Number of rooms after** 5 **Number of apartments** 1 **Number of residents** 3 **Address** Fahndorf 63, 3710 Weinviertel, Austria

The scale and geometry of the new addition allows for a natural integration into the context, while the outer skin of thick untreated aluminum panels creates a confident contrast.

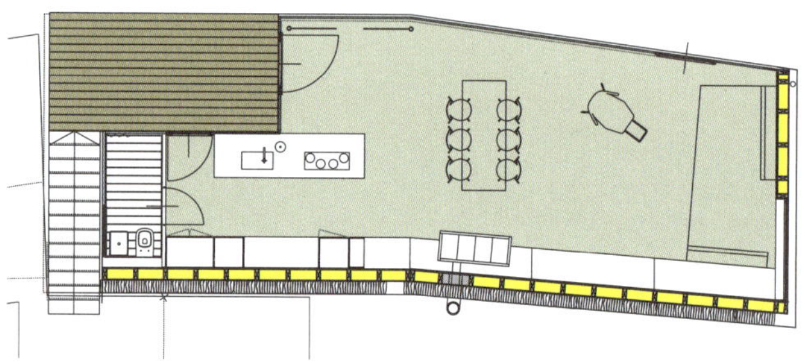

Ground floor plan

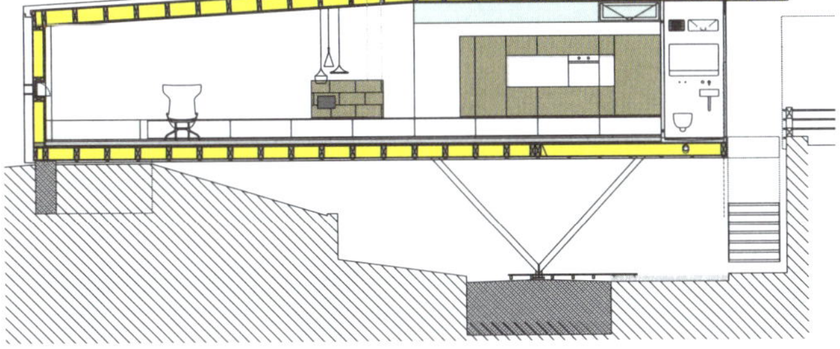

Section

This project involved the creation of affordable housing units in an old school building in the municipality of Essômes sur Marne, France. The original distribution of the building has been entirely reorganized and reconceptualized for disabled persons. Panels of Corten steel mark the new main entrance and the openings give the project a strikingly contemporary feel. The new entrance hall with a core staircase has been created in place of the previous technical rooms. A new distribution is recognizable on the main elevation aligned with the adjacent road. The new parts are emphasized by meticulously finished raw materials, which give the whole design a much-needed contemporary character. Inside, the reflections of the natural surroundings coming through the bay window create a pleasant and calm atmosphere in the communal parts of the building.

19th century → 2017

For this school conversion housing units take shape in what was once a former educational building.

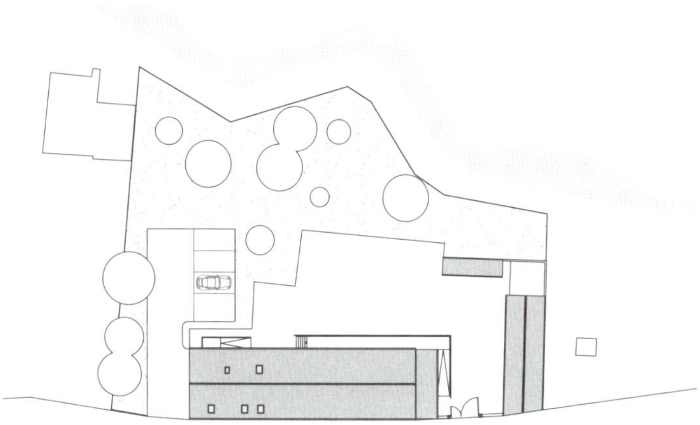

Site plan

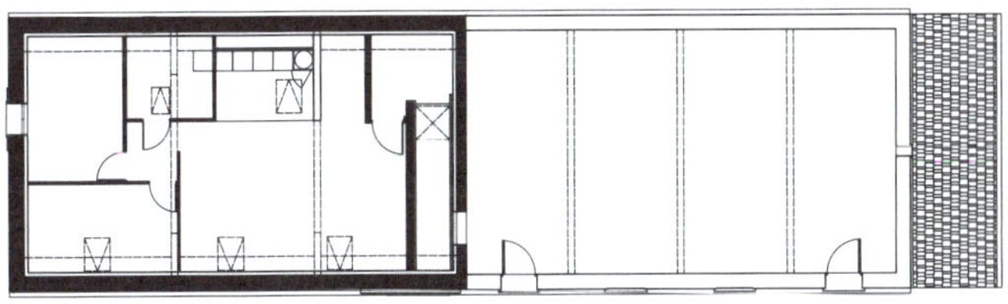

Attic floor plan

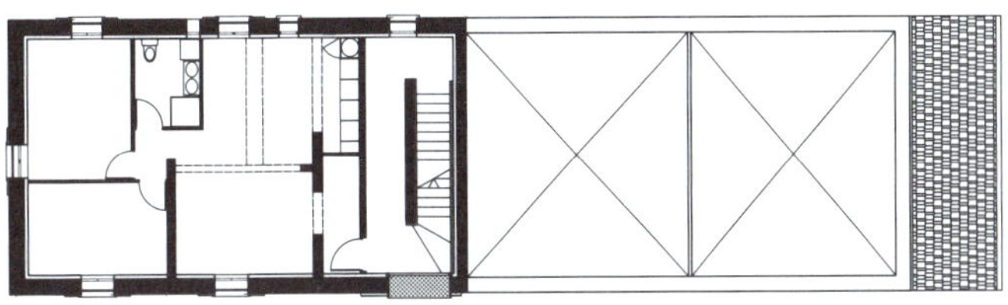

First floor plan

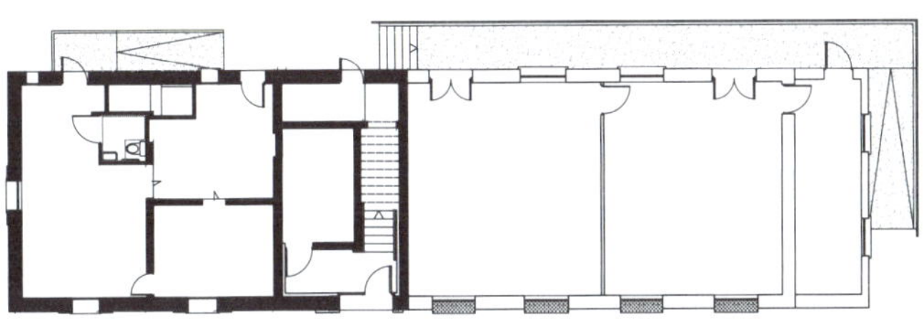

Ground floor plan

Architect ACBS Architectes **Completion** 2017 **Original building** School, 19th century **Gross floor area** 455 m^2 **Number of rooms before** 12 **Number of rooms after** 15 **Number of apartments** 2 **Address** Essômes sur Marne, France

The composition preserves the simplicity and authenticity of the original building.

1990s → 2014

This old warehouse has been transformed into the Unforgettable House in Pohang.

This project involved the conversion of an old warehouse into housing. The design is based on the idea of a "house in a house". As there was enough height for two floors, a kitchen, dining room, living room and a small hidden library have been established on the ground floor, while the family room, bathroom, dressing room, and bedroom are all located on the first floor. The wall in the common space was finished with plywood and the lighting elements were designed to accentuate the warmth of the wood. Other spaces have been painted in white to induce a calm atmosphere. The floor is finished with white tiles to create a bright space. By leaving most of the rough concrete exterior wall untouched, the architects were also responsible for the mural, inspired by a barcode.

Architect studio GAON **Completion** 2014 **Original building** Warehouse, early 1990s **Gross floor area before** 198 m² **Gross floor area after** 250 m² **Number of rooms before** 1 **Number of rooms after** 6 **Number of apartments** 1 **Number of residents** 2 **Address** Imjung-ri, Jangi-myeon, Pohang, Gyeongsang-do, South Korea

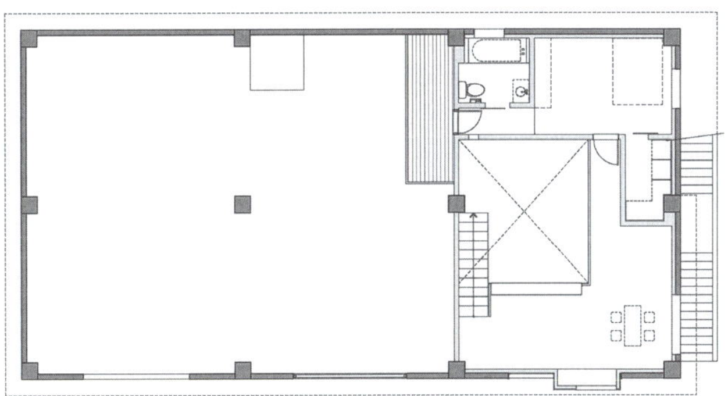

First floor plan

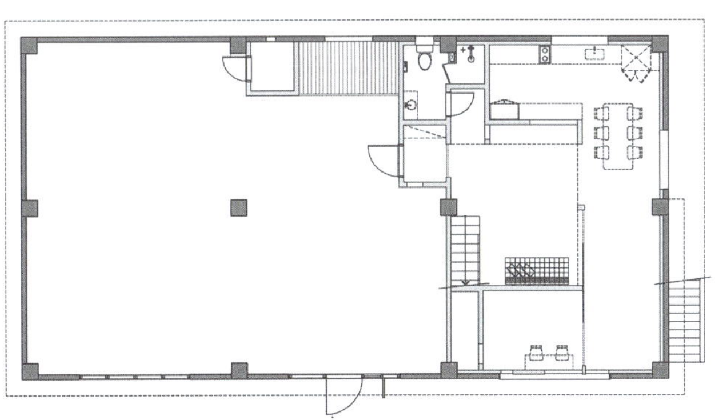

Ground floor plan

Plain colors and wood give a warm and bright atmosphere to the house surrounded by nature.

1939/1980 → 2016

Chokladfabriken transformed a contemporary factory into residential units.

This project involved the transformation of a former chocolate factory and an attached office building into housing units. Following the closure of the factory, the building was converted into offices with a 23-meter-deep extension added to the west. The extension was connected to the staircase of the factory building but was set back six meters from the street frontage. The architects retained this structure and aligned the façade with the neighboring buildings. The apartments facing only the street receive additional daylight through atriums cut out of the original slabs. These atriums are open to the sky and provide daylight and fresh air. The façade of the former factory has been restored to its original condition, while the former office extension now has a new single-glazed façade that provides the atrium apartments with unheated conservatories.

Architect Jägnefält Milton **Completion** 2016 **Original building** Factory by Axel Sjögren, 1939; office by Lars Carlsson, 1980 **Gross floor area before** 6,300 m² **Gross floor area after** 7,700 m² **Number of apartments** 85 **Number of residents** 150–200 **Address** Industrigatan, 2, 11246 Stockholm, Sweden

Light-flooded atrium apartments adapt to the structure of the former factory.

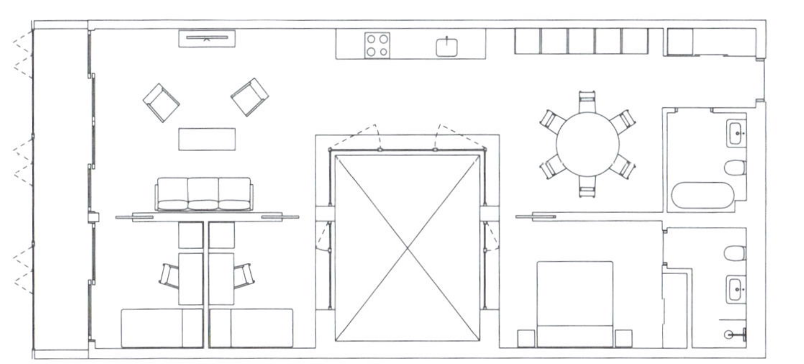

Ground floor plan

1958 → 2012

This project involved converting a former atelier into Meisenrain 39, an attractive and inviting family home.

In 1958 renowned architects Brennerstuhl and Neuenschwander built an atelier for advertising consultants V.N. Cohen in Gockhausen. The building has an unusual design that has retained its architectural relevance even today. The renovation to a single-family home was carried out in 2012, and the 70-square-meter ground floor space was transformed into a living, dining and kitchen area. The sideboards in front of the windows are directly connected to the built-in sofa in the living room, which is interrupted by the large chimney. The stairway provides a spatial connection between the ground and basement levels. The bedrooms have also been fitted with continuous sideboards beneath the windows. The flooring comprises patterned stone slabs and these have also been used on the walls of the wet room. The white-plastered walls and ceilings have been painted a light beige shade, complemented by the brown curtains. The light green accents on the inside of the X-shaped concrete columns create an exciting play of colors.

Architect Dolenc Scheiwiller Architekten and Beat Nievergelt Architekt **Completion** 2012 **Original building** Atelier, 1958 **Gross floor area** 190 m² **Number of rooms** 3 **Number of apartments** 1 **Number of residents** 2 **Address** Meisenrain 39, 8044 Gockhausen, Switzerland

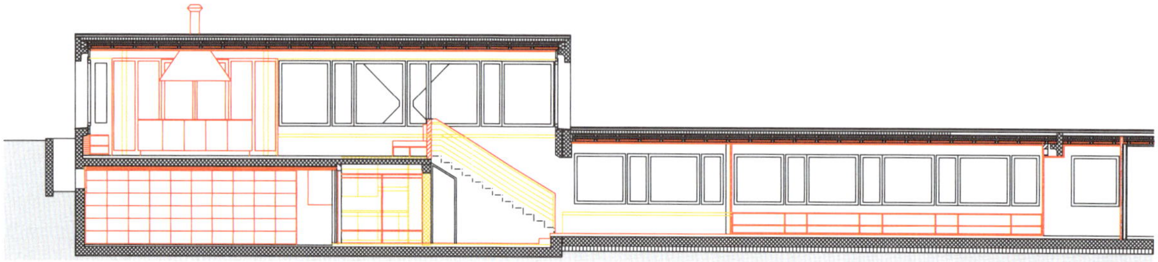

Section

Bright and open rooms ensure a welcoming and idyllic family home in the countryside.

In the Regional Natural Park of Boucles de la Seine, a ruined barn has been converted into a place of residence. Abandoned at the edge of the river, it used to hold the fodder for the work horses. Its thin weatherboarding had worn away over time and only the timber framework remained. In this very simple, rural context, the project intends to be just as rustic, without sophistication or details. The new shelter was built onto the existing one. A shell of zinc covers the roof and walls to conserve a monolithic, agricultural architecture with few openings. The framework is the fundamental element of the new residence. From the outside, it remains partially visible, beneath the zinc envelope, thus conferring an incomplete aspect to the construction, as though eroded by the surrounding nature. The windows and doors are visually understated: the archetypal house has been kept at bay to give rise to another kind of habitat.

1920 → 2016

The Barn demonstrates how a former ruin can be revived without losing its rustic charm.

Architect Antonin Ziegler architecte **Completion** 2016 **Original building** Barn, before 1920 **Gross floor area before** 180 m² **Gross floor area after** 220 m² **Number of rooms** 5 **Number of apartments** 1 **Number of residents** 5 **Address** Notre-Dame-de-Bliquetuit, France

Playing with the sense of incompleteness this project makes a bold statement.

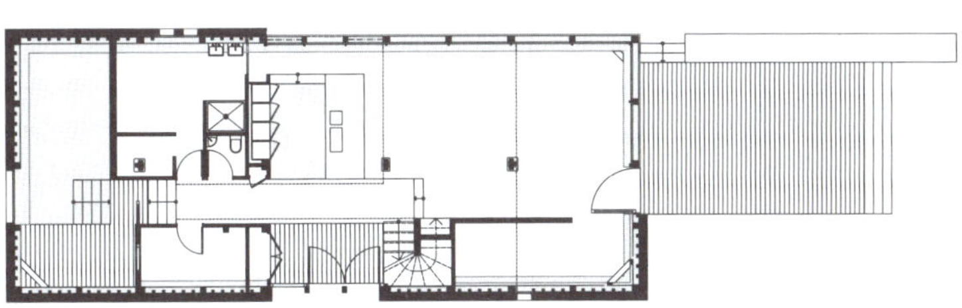

Ground floor plan

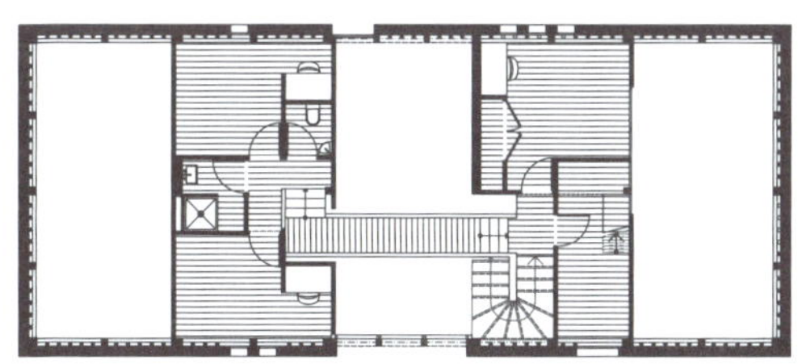

First floor plan

1920s → 2015

The Wyeth Residences show the conversion of an old school.

The Wyeth Residences are an adaptive reuse project of two early 20th-century school buildings in Cambridge, MA, that were converted into multifamily housing units. Today, the LEED Platinum certified building stands adorned with its salvaged original brickwork. Reclaimed building elements, such as the existing wood, roof rafters and masonry were repurposed for the interior finishes and the overall core and shell. Due to the existing tall floor-to-floor ceiling heights intermediate floors were able to be added into the middle of the building and extend to the exterior walls. The resulting relationship of the interior floors and exterior masonry openings created a dynamic façade pattern of windows and offset balconies. The existing shell and sectional qualities provided unique characteristics of interior and exterior space for the units.

Architect Touloukian Touloukian **Landscape architect** Crosby, Schlessinger, Smallridge **Completion** 2015 **Original building** Catholic high school, 1920s **Gross floor area before** 5,050 m² **Gross floor area after** 5,388 m² **Number of rooms before** 30 **Number of rooms after** 50 **Number of apartments** 44 **Number of residents** 92 **Address** Rindge Avenue 120, Cambridge, MA 02140, USA

Second floor plan

First floor plan

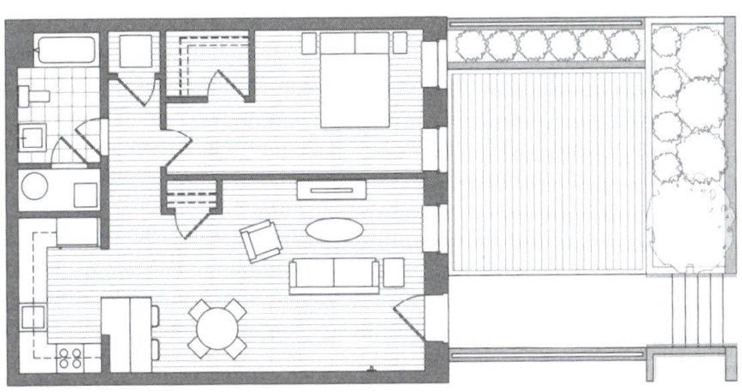

Ground floor plan

Driven by sustainability as a primary focal point, dynamic façades and original brickwork retain the building's identity.

The Casa Estudio combines the revitalization of an industrial building with a cunning design for a small budget.

This functional work-living space is located in a micro industrial area of Querétaro City. The regeneration project revived a building dating back to the 1980s. Intersticial Arquitectura chose to approach the run-down structure by understanding the pre-existing conditions. This led to the insertion of subtle interventions including the system of overlapping patios and straightforward construction methods. In turn, the series of patios allow for the house to be naturally ventilated and flooded with natural light. Meanwhile, clay and concrete were chosen to line the walls as these are local materials that create a sense of strength and contrast. The main challenge was to do more with less: to provide an architectural solution that extends a studio space on the ground floor, separates this from the a new apartment on the first floor, and to maximize the living space, inside and out.

Architect Intersticial Arquitectura **Completion** 2016 **Original building** Industrial building, 1980 **Gross floor area** 160 m² **Number of rooms before** 2 **Number of rooms after** 3 **Number of residents** 2 + 8 employees **Address** Querétaro, Mexico

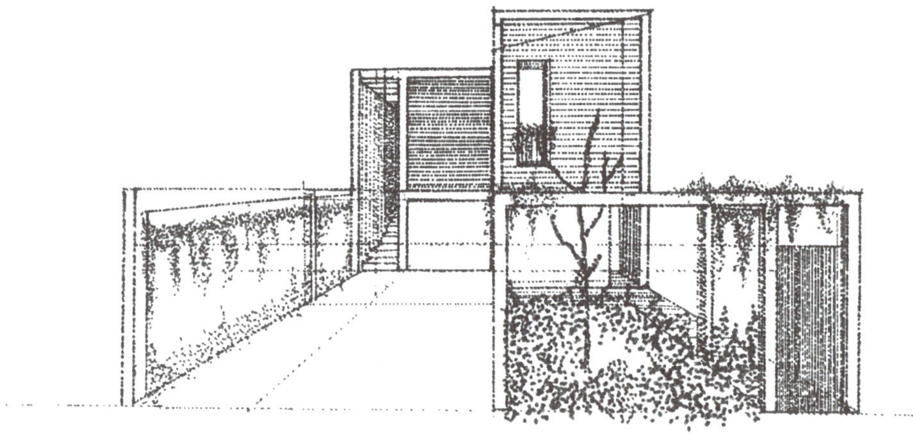

Ground floor plan

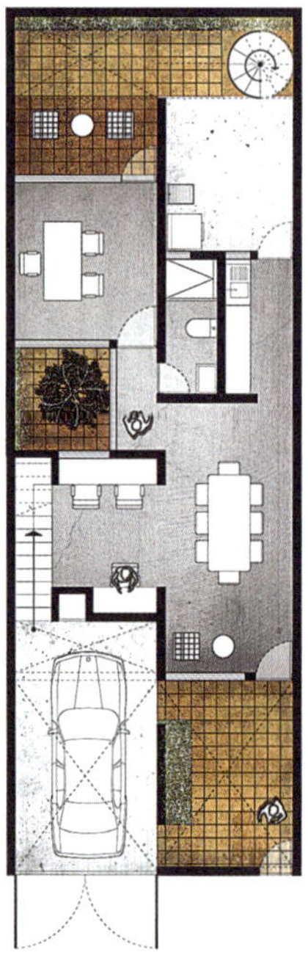

First floor plan

The choice of materials respects the architectural history and its limitations, without lacking a sense of singularity.

1863 → 2013

In this transformation of a former gypsum factory, 19th-century industrial architecture and the creation of flexible living space fuse in an extraordinary manner.

This conversion of a gypsum factory into a residential complex with a restaurant and yacht pier was conducted in two phases. The factory is a typical example of brick architecture of Riga in the end of the 19th century, with splendid brick details and textures, interesting wooden constructions, characteristic window rhythm and organization. The complex now offers residential space of different types – from small one-bedroom studios to spacious separate houses with three or four levels. Most of the apartments have outdoor spaces – French balconies, roof terraces, verandas, wooden decks. The interior design preserves the rough textures and patina of the original brick, metal and wooden constructions. Mainly natural materials have been used – old pine plank floors, specifically designed hexagonal concrete tiles, as well as wooden window frames, windowsills, doors, metal staircases and banisters.

Architect Zaigas Gailes Birojs **Completion** 2013 **Original building** Gypsum factory, 1863 **Gross floor area before** 5,542 m² **Gross floor area after** 11,594 m² **Number of apartments** 97 **Address** Balasta dambis 70/72, LV-1048, Riga, Latvia

Preserving the characteristic industrial elements helped to build up a visual relationship to the past without abandoning the amenities of modern life.

Ground floor plan

1920 → 2014

Pavillon d'éte – transforming a small brick shack into a modern home.

This project aimed to transform a shack into modern accommodation. The original shed had a high ceiling and featured a large archway that sought to establish a connection between the inside and outside areas. To maintain the original spatial dimensions, the project has adapted to make the best possible use of the existing space, altering the volume as little as possible. Occupying the upper volume of the shed, the new intervention is hidden from view by wickerwork screens. Wickerwork, a material designers commonly use for chairs, has been given a new purpose.
On the ground floor, the kitchen and the bathroom have been partitioned off. In the living room, thanks to an ample curtain, it is possible to shower in a vast open space, while enjoying expansive views of the natural environment. Thus, the exceptional rapport between the inside and outside of the shelter has been preserved.

Architect Agence Noémie Meney **Completion** 2014 **Original building** Garden storage, 1920 **Gross floor area before** 16 m² **Gross floor area after** 21 m² **Number of rooms** 1 **Number of apartments** 1 **Number of residents** 2 **Address** 83680 La Garde, France

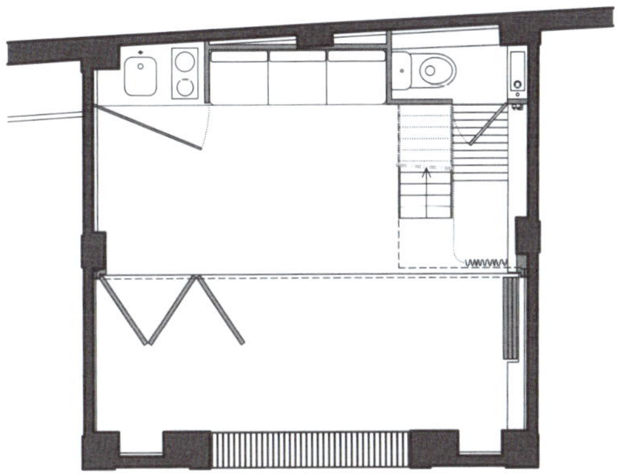

Ground floor plan

Section

Elevation

Using wickerwork and a floating room concept, this ensemble becomes one with its surroundings.

1889 → 2017

Oeconomie-gebäude Josef Weiss offers new living space in place of an old stable building.

This building was built in 1889 and originally served as an extension of the hotel building and the Josef Weiss wine cellar in the Dornbirn railway quarter. The building was listed as a historical monument in 1997 and thus managed to avoid demolition. A number of suggestions were made about what to do with the old building but none were realized. The clients finally bought the structure in 2016 and carefully renovated it, creating an apartment and atelier. A key aspect of the project was the preservation and restoration of various original elements, such as parts of the old stable, floor and coach house. A loft-like apartment has been created with split-levels, flexible spaces and intimate loft rooms. The façade has been preserved; the renovation work was carried out from the inside. A small veranda is located inside the façade, offering a covered area. Slits in the façade draw light inside and offer views. The original floorboards were numbered, cleaned and then put back in place and restored timber elements are now visible.

Architect Julia Kick Architektin **Completion** 2017 **Original building** Horse barn, remise, hay store, 1889 **Gross floor area** 230 m² **Number of rooms** 4 **Number of apartments** 1 **Number of residents** 2 **Address** Dornbirn, Austria

This inviting building impresses with its natural wood look, which creates a cozy and warm atmosphere.

Initially, this first-floor studio apartment was a dark and poorly planned space with a narrow living area and a ladder-accessed sleeping platform. Adding a large window on the eastern façade brought in much-needed morning light. Installing folding full-height partitions maintained the open-plan character, while enabling the creation of a generous master bedroom. Extending the mezzanine and replacing the ladder with a staircase resulted in a larger, more private guest sleeping area. By subdividing the existing bathroom, a new en suite, a guest toilet and a dressing room have been established. To minimize costs, the existing dark timber floors were painted with a black-and-white chequerboard pattern, enhancing the perceived width of the room. The kitchen, relocated beneath the new window, was constructed on site from birch-faced plywood. A room-brightening white-oil finish that left the grain exposed made a textural connection to the original brickwork and timber planks still visible beneath the paint.

1876 → 1900 → 1987 → 2013

City View House has undergone several architectural developments, from a school and bakery to a trendy living space.

Ground floor plans after transformation

Ground floor plans before transformation

Adding full-height folding partitions helped to restructure the ensemble, while the reinterpretation of the original timber boards recalls the space's history.

Architect Russian For Fish **Completion** 2013 **Original building** School around 1876, bakery around 1900, transformed into flats in 1987 **Gross floor area before** 75 m² **Gross floor area after** 79 m² **Number of rooms after** 1 **Number of apartments** 1 **Number of residents** 2 **Address** Bethnal Green, London, UK

1890 → 2013

The Fire House turned a fire station into housing.

The project included the conversion of a fire house from the 19th century. The architects have transformed the ground floor studio into a photo studio for the current owner, who works as a photographer. The second floor houses living areas and the third floor is a penthouse that includes a master suite, lounge and a rooftop garden. The main objective of this project was to achieve a balance of privacy and natural light. This is most apparent in the case of a light well that penetrates the house from the new third floor roof down to the center of the second floor, flooding the kitchen with daylight. A bridge passes through this sky-lit space and connects the lounge to the master bedroom suite. The walled-in rooftop garden is configured to wrap around the corner of the penthouse to allow for rooftop strolls.

Architect TBD Architecture and Design Studio **Completion** 2013 **Original building** Fire house, 1890 **Gross floor area before** 370 m² **Gross floor area after** 453 m² **Number of rooms before** 3 **Number of rooms after** 10 **Number of apartments** 1 **Number of residents** 3 **Address** Scholes Street, Brooklyn, NY, USA

The former fire house now serves as a private living space bathed in light.

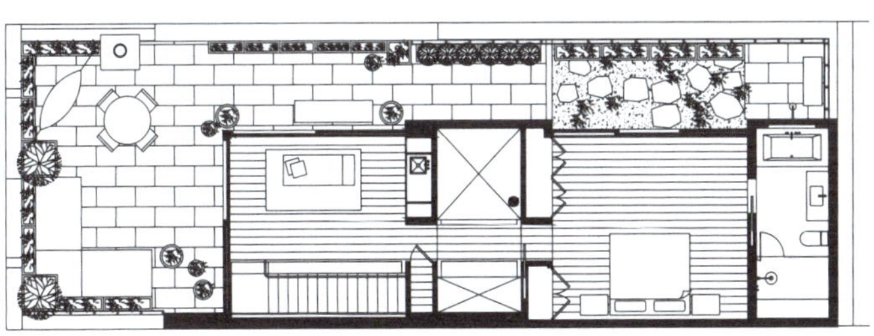

Third floor plan

1870 → 2011

Maina demonstrates how the historic beauty of a traditional settlement and ecological living can work together.

Nestled in a quaint village of traditional stone towers in Eastern Mani, this hillside house offers stunning views of the countryside, looking out over olive groves and the sea. Originally an abandoned megalithic two-story building dating from the 19th century, the house is surrounded by a garden with olive trees, carob trees and prickly pears, as well as a cave. To the east, the yard abuts a 16th-century tower, and just below there is a Byzantine chapel with 12th-century frescos. The original building was maintained as a long narrow volume, which unfolds perpendicularly to the topographic contour lines of the hillside. The new addition comprised a second long narrow volume added adjacent to this old building. This transformation by architect Elena Zervoudakis preserved the building's traditional elements and combined them with minimalist interiors to give a sense of serenity and primordial spirit.

Architect Z-level architecture **Completion** 2011 **Original building** Traditional settlement, 1870 **Gross floor area before** 88 m^2 **Gross floor area after** 150 m^2 **Number of rooms before** 2 **Number of rooms after** 4 **Number of apartments** 2 **Number of residents** 8–10 **Address** Exo Nyfi, Mani, Greece

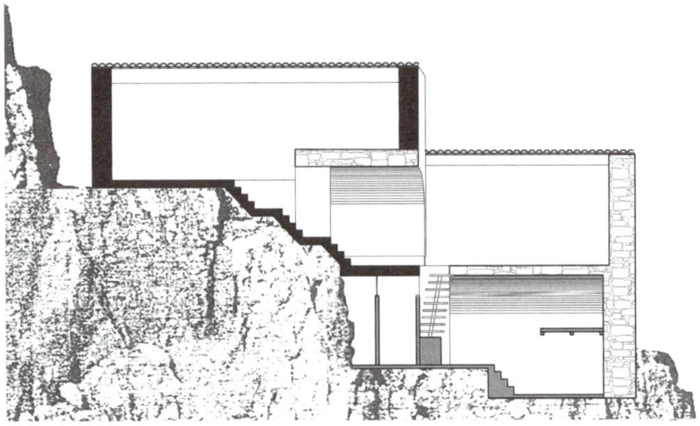

Section

Ground floor plan

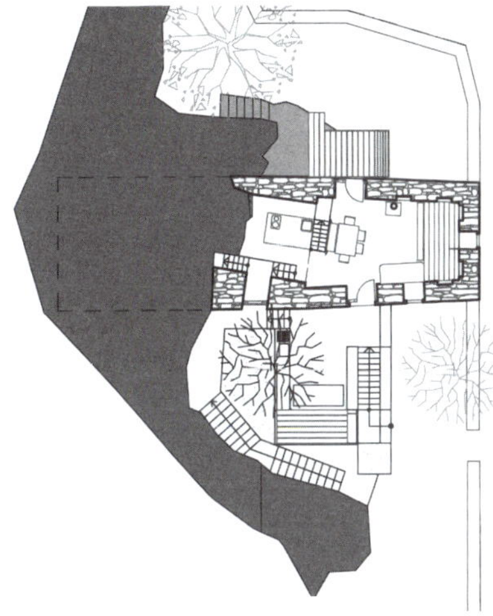

First floor plan

By preserving the historic surroundings and using local materials, a sustainable and esthetic ensemble has been created, determined by the dynamic interaction between past and present.

1960s → 2014

The Gables project involved the transformation of a mechanic's garage into housing.

What was once a mechanic's garage and office building now houses a small housing complex. Externally the buildings have been refaced, uniting what was previously a patchwork arrangement into a balanced composition. The predominant material in the courtyard is brick, used on the rear façades of the Victorian terrace. The architects chose to establish a stronger connection between the development and its surroundings, picking up on the ornate rendered front elevation. A dark insulating render has been used along the rear elevation and introduced asymmetrical gables to the front-facing elevations. Brick is also the predominant material inside offering a striking contrast to the concrete finishes, coffered ceiling and oak paneling. The open floor plan is structured by large openings that draw natural daylight inside.

The use of brick as the main material is a reference to the building's history, while the asymmetrical gables give each building its own identity.

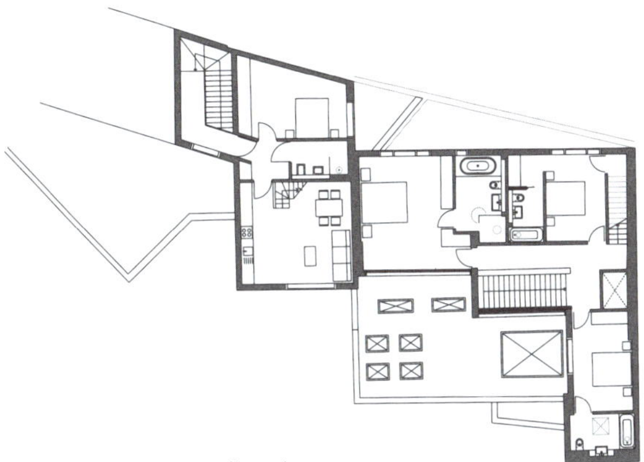

First floor plan

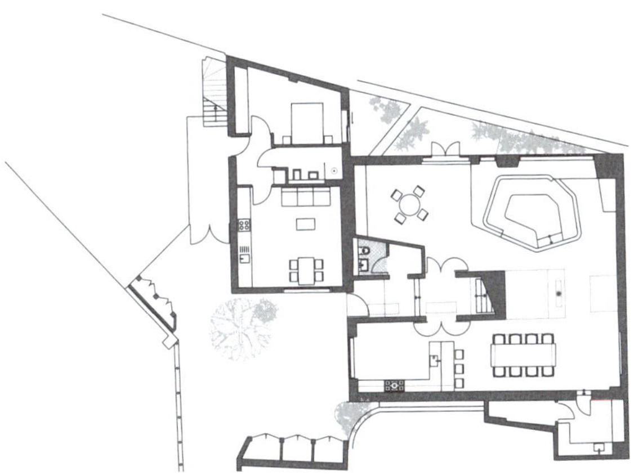

Ground floor plan

Architect Patalab Architecture **Completion** 2014 **Original building** Mechanic's garage, 1960s **Gross floor area before** 350 m² **Gross floor area after** 365 m² **Number of rooms before** 4 **Number of rooms after** 8 **Number of apartments** 3 **Address** Primrose Hill, London, UK

1928 → 2018

This design breathes new life into Halle 17.

The new Clouth quarter is located in Nippes, a lively city quarter on the edge of Cologne's inner city. The listed building Halle 17, commissioned by Instone Real Estate, graces the centrally located Luftschiffplatz. The 125-meter-long and 35-meter-wide former production hall is a monument to 19th-century Rhenisch industrial culture and forms the backbone of urban city planning for this area. This project involved the creation of a flexible program of apartments, commercial units and restaurants. A key focus of the design was the preservation of the brick façade and part of the historical steel lattice formwork. Two access points connect Halle 17 with the adjacent streets and Luftschiffplatz, thus structuring the building interior into six segments. The northerly part of the building houses a toy workshop for children, restaurants and apartments, while the other segments house larger apartments which offer space for both working and living.

Architect Jürgensen & Jürgensen Architekten **Completion** 2018 **Original building** Industrial building, 1928 **Gross floor area before** 6,500 m² **Gross floor area after** 15,272 m² **Number of apartments** 47 **Number of residents** Approx. 150 **Address** Luftschiffplatz 1–66, 50733 Cologne, Germany

A witness to Cologne's historical roots, this industrial shell wraps around modern residential units.

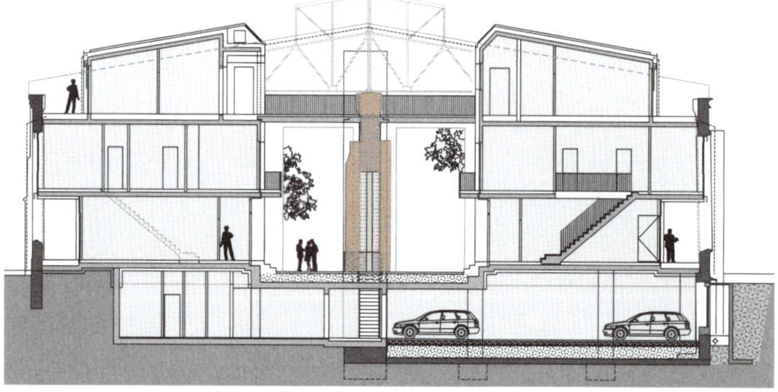

Section

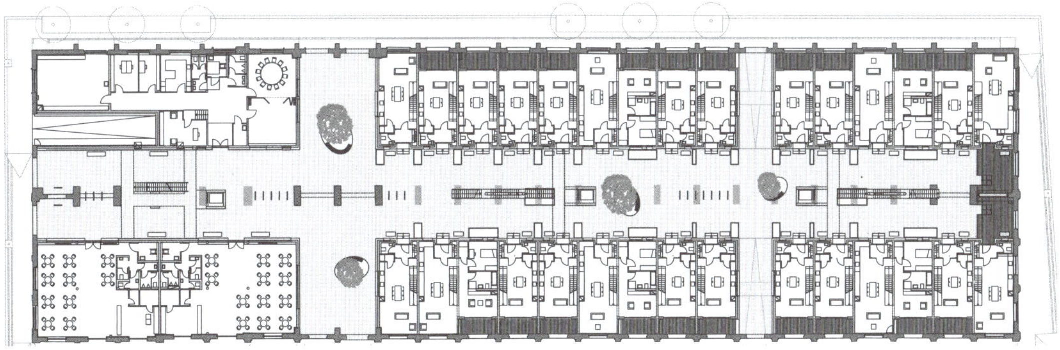

Floor plan whole complex

1929 → 2016

House Leopold brought back to life by the insertion of a former woodshed to create a classy yet innovative living environment.

In the 1950s, this villa served as a weekend house for a middle-class family in post-war Austria. The complex was formerly composed of the main building and a little woodshed. Over the past few decades these structures have lost their original purpose. To revive the ensemble, the shed and the house were connected by a hovering larch deck that functions as an open living room and offers views across the garden. Around the old apple trees, circles were cut out of the deck. When the children look out of the window they see the tops of the fruit trees, illuminated from below at night. The ground floor is still used for storing garden tools, while the upstairs has been made snug and comfortable. Spotlights illuminate the brass in the evening, creating a warm light – even in freezing winter.

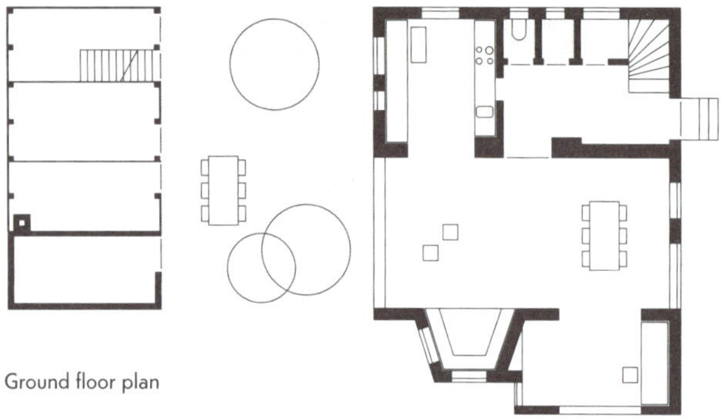

Ground floor plan

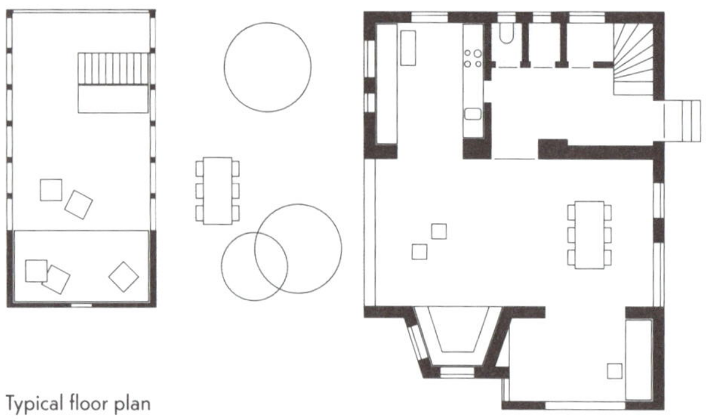

Typical floor plan

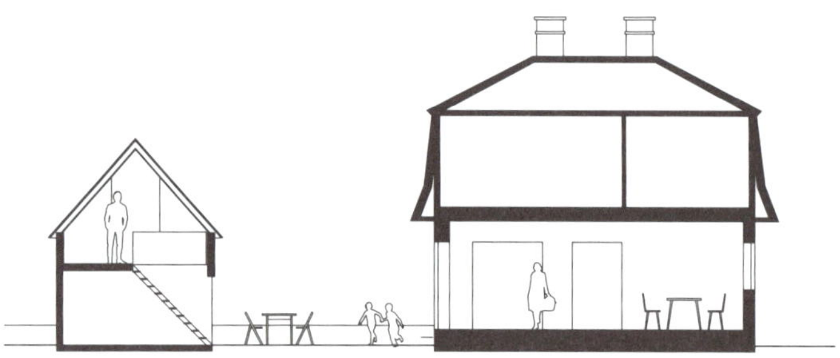

Section

Connecting the separate parts helped to create an extraordinary design that is embedded in the existing landscape and establishes an almost enchanted atmosphere.

Architect Franz&Sue **Completion** 2016 **Original building** Woodshed, 1929 **Gross floor area** Main building: 155 m², woodshed: 60 m² **Number of rooms before** Main building: 3, woodshed: 4 **Number of rooms after** Main building: 2, woodshed: 5 **Number of apartments** 1 **Address** Eichgraben, Austria

The upper level of the old barn was originally used as a hay barn, while the lower level served as a stable for goats and sheep. A contemporary wooden annex has been added to extend the space and enable the transformation of the building into a family home. The barn was completely emptied and a reinforced concrete structure built in order to meet the region's structural and seismic requirements. Interior thermal insulation has been carefully added to ensure the preservation of the barn's original exterior. The insertion of large windows into the masonry respects the architectural history, replacing some timber sections with glass. The backbone of this house is the solid larch staircase that allows light and sound to travel from one floor to the other. The wooden furniture was designed by Ralph Germann architectes and reinforces the coherence of the design.

1920 → 2016

Transforming this barn into House EKC ensures comfort, while respecting the architectural tradition of the building.

Architect Ralph Germann architectes **Completion** 2016 **Original building** Barn, approx. 1920 **Gross floor area before** 70 m² **Gross floor area after** 200 m² **Number of rooms before** 1 **Number of rooms after** 6 **Number of apartments** 1 **Number of residents** 5 **Address** Orsières, Switzerland

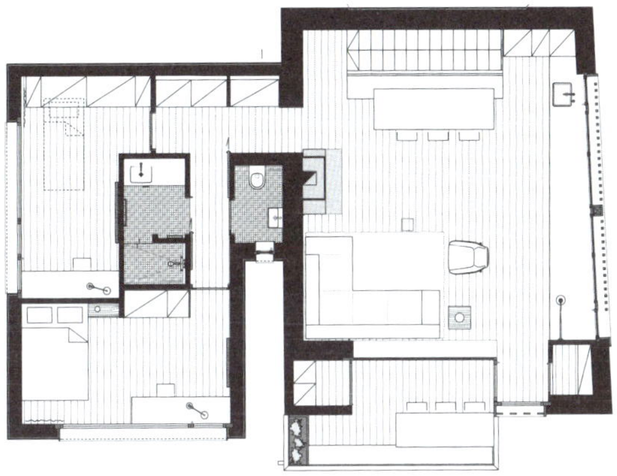

Mezzanine plan

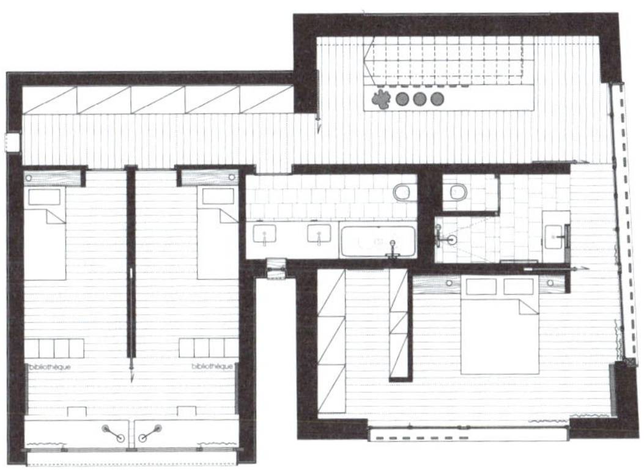

First floor plan

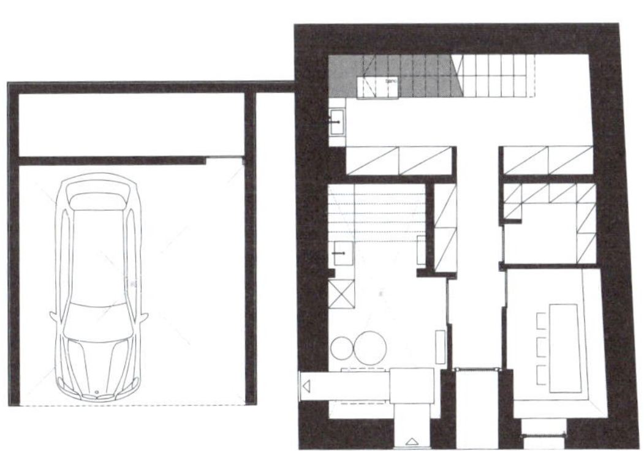

Ground floor plan

Adapting the preexisting structure helped to preserve the original charm.

Until recently, these rooms housed the workshop and garage of a motorbike enthusiast. The single-story construction has undergone a complete renovation inside. The reduced design offers space for robust materials, such as oak flooring, natural stone in the main bathroom and black linoleum for all of the built-in elements. The space facing the courtyard houses the kitchen and dining area, and behind these are the bedrooms and guest area with en suite bathrooms. Light is drawn into this part of the apartment via new skylights and additional light shafts. The daylight provides the apartment a comfortable atmosphere, while the built-in air conditioning system ensures optimal temperature.

1960 → 2014

Once a garage the Loftgebäude Sendling now offers comfortable living space.

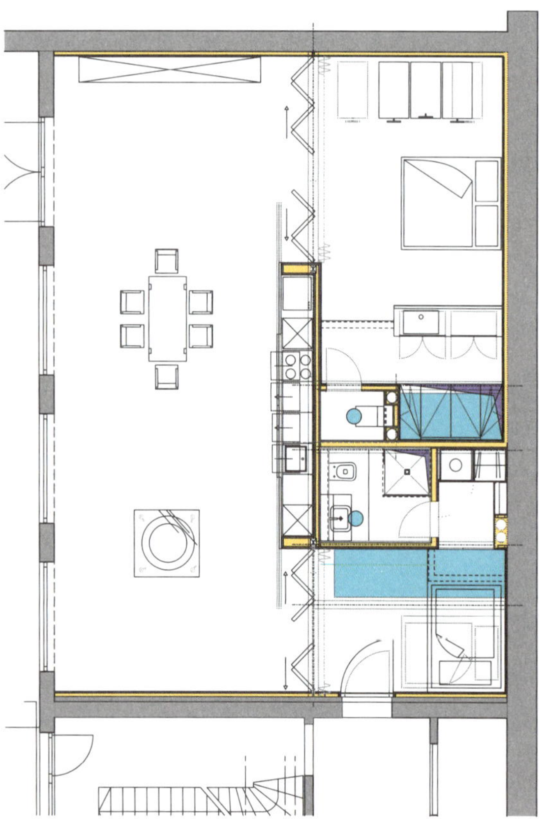

Ground floor plan

The new accommodation is determined by a reduced design and rough materials, thus recalling the pragmatic functionalism of the preexisting structure.

Architect Marie Aigner **Completion** 2014 **Original building** Garage, approx. 1950–1960 **Gross floor area** 145 m² **Number of rooms** 3 **Number of apartments** 1 **Address** Sendling, Munich, Germany

The designers faced the challenge of transforming a former stable into a residential property complete with study. The final structure comprised living space for a three-person family and a home office along with the other necessary rooms. It is located on a site at the end of a valley and is surrounded by woodland. It was desired that the material chosen for the façade and roof should blend esthetically with the adjacent forest. The external façade was clad in vertical strips of blackened fir, echoing the nearby tree trunks, while the intensively greened roof surface mirrors the woodland foliage. The long, narrow form of the building allows the two distinct functions of the interior to emerge clearly. Passing through the entrance, the visitor encounters the office space, its walls as high as the building itself and the necessary workplaces integrated into a gallery level. The adjoining rooms are reached via the former feeding area, while the living space is located in the rear section of the building.

1950s → 2012

Once a horse stable, the House Stable complex now serves as exceptional environment suitable for living and working.

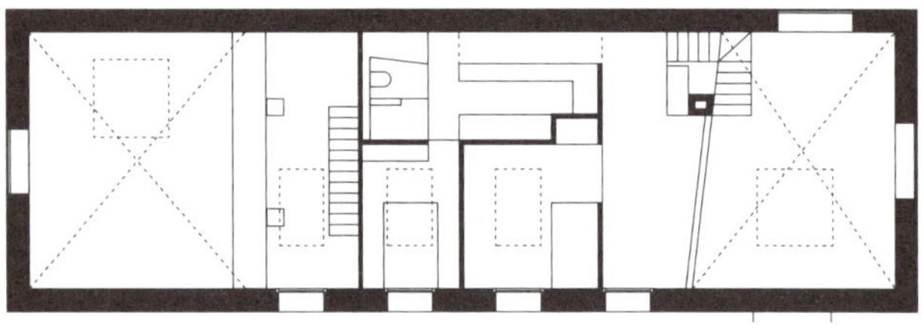

First floor plan

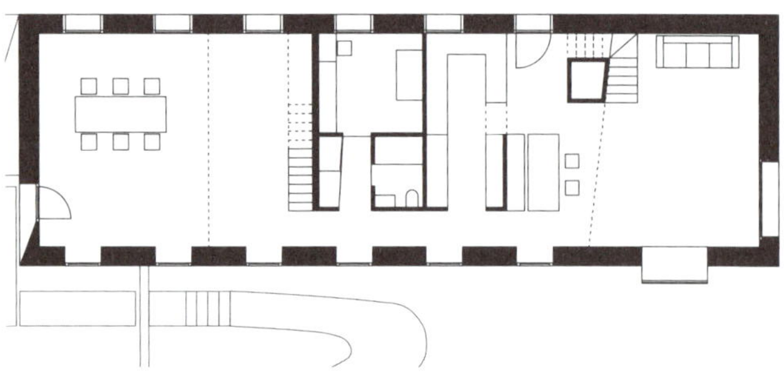

Ground floor plan

Using blackened fir supports a harmonious integration of the new ensemble by echoing the nearby forest.

Architect stocker.dewes architekten **Completion** 2012 **Original building** Stable, late 1950s **Gross floor area before** 240 m² **Gross floor area after** 200 m² **Number of rooms** 2 **Number of apartments** 1 **Address** Freiburg, Germany

This design breathes new life into former mid-century cylindrical grain silos. As much of the original outer silo esthetic as possible was recreated as most of the old structures had to be dismantled due to their poor condition. This reimagining allowed for a vast variety of layouts within; from smart one-bedroom flats to three-level lofts. The round silo structures have been utilized as balcony zones that extend the apartments. A mainly rectangular dark extension expands the silo structure naturally within the reimagined plot. The first two of the thirteen floors consist of neo-lofts with galleries. In keeping with the original industrial atmosphere of the area, the raw, in-situ cast concrete surfaces are a vivid element throughout the interior of the building. This re-use project is a fine example of how an area of cultural importance can be reimagined without losing its character.

1960 → 2014

The Tervahovi Silos project involved the development of a culturally important complex, combined with futuristic living spaces.

Architect PAVE Architects **Completion** 2014 **Original building** Industrial grain silo by SOK (The Central Finnish Cooperative Society), 1960 **Gross floor area before** 520 m² **Gross floor area after** 10,805 m² **Number of apartments** 95 **Number of residents** 220 **Address** Siilotie 21, 90520 Oulu, Finland

The reinterpretation of the former silo structure led to the fusion of industrial pragmatism and residential comfort.

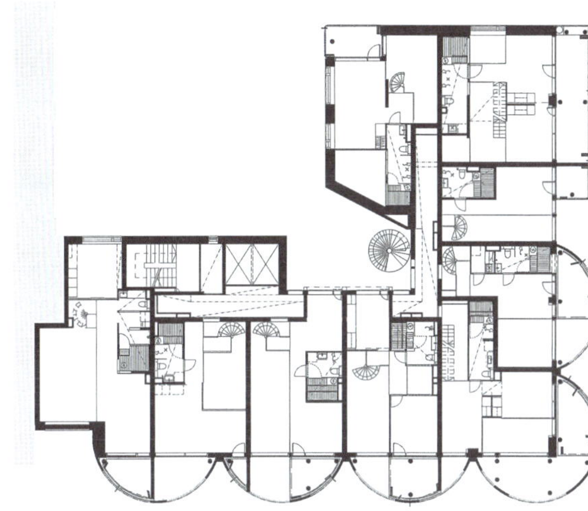

Gallery floor plan

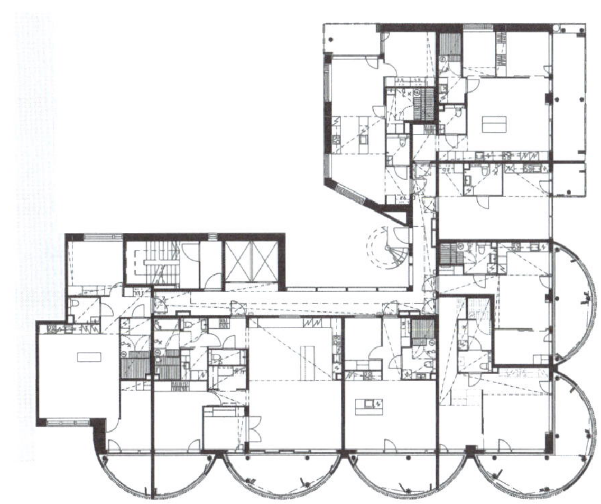

Typical floor plan

1910 → 2017

Inspired by the movie "Reservoir Dogs", this industrial building has been transformed into a comfortable home.

This unusual project is an adaptive reuse of a listed industrial building into housing in Hamilton's North End waterfront neighborhood, and part of the legacy of Hamilton's storied industrial history. The architects renovated the vacant industrial building into three large residential loft-style townhouses. The design inspiration was the similarity to the warehouse setting of the "Reservoir Dogs" movie by Quentin Tarantino. The finished product is a highly individualized design with customization and detailing of each dwelling, both inside and out. Colors, cabinets, finishes, lighting, and landscaping are all unique. Remnants of the past industrial history have been left intact as far as possible throughout the whole complex. The exterior design blends the historic character with modern steel, glass block, corrugated metal siding and custom-designed steel and glass elements.

Architect TCA / Thier + Curran Architects **Completion** 2017 **Original building** Jobborn machine and tool fabrication shop, 1910 **Gross floor area before** 420.35 m² **Number of rooms before** 4 **Number of rooms after** 14 **Number of apartments** 3 **Number of residents** 8 **Address** 7-9-11 Brock Street, Hamilton L8L 4L5, Canada

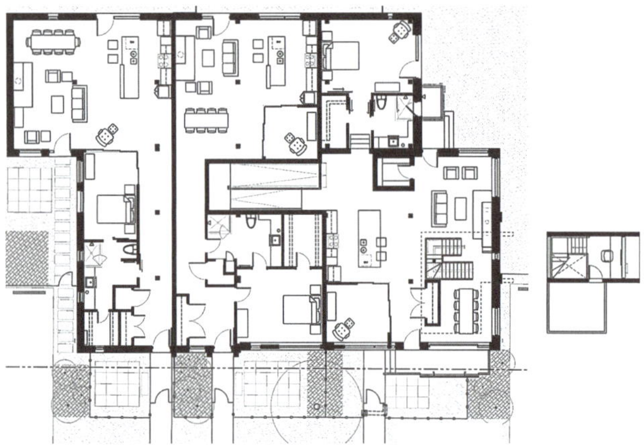

Ground floor plan

The individualized design of the open rooms preserves the industrial character of the building.

19th century → 2017

With Beacon Loft, a unique mixture of styles has been established in what was once a 19th-century textile factory.

Located on the top floor of what was originally a 19th-century textile factory in Beacon, New York, this project involved the creation of six condo units in 2016 with the goal to maintain as much of the original structure as possible, including brick walls, oversized windows, beams and steel components. Stylistically, the aim was to layer historic Americana design with elements of art deco and rock and roll. In order to create a look that was both eclectic yet unified, the space was grounded with a neutral color palette accented with deep blues, golden tones and rich woods. Throughout the home, new paint, wallpaper and lighting add drama and create unique spaces. Each space also blends a myriad of antique and vintage pieces alongside contemporary ones to add a sense of heritage amid modern design. Finally, bold art selections add depth and dimension to the soaring walls.

Architect Grisoro Designs **Completion** 2017 **Original building** Textile factory, 19th century **Gross floor area** 3,150 m² **Number of rooms** 6 **Address** 11 Creek Drive, Beacon, NY 12508, USA

Preserving as much as possible, but still allowing old and new to fuse together to form a rough and yet elegant setting inspired by industrial functionality.

Set amongst beech-wooded farmland, this project was used as an agricultural threshing and cattle barn until the mid-1990s. Built in traditional brick and flint, the barn was enlarged to twice its original size thanks to a Victorian addition in 1864 – resulting in the building which stands today. The project involved significant restructuring and reservicing of the barn. With the removal of many structural walls, floors and beams a complicated package of concealed steelwork and structural timber framing had to be added. Spatially, the changes resulted in two large living areas. The opening up of the south end of the barn created a vast double-height open-plan living room, rising up to the rafters of the main roof and into the gable ends of the transepts on either side. At the north end a dedicated library and music listening room has been created. A new moveable staircase was fabricated from black steel and now functions as connecting eye-catcher.

Architect McLaren Excell **Completion** 2011 **Original building** Barn, late 18th century **Gross floor area before** 516 m² **Gross floor area after** 476 m² **Number of rooms before** 25 **Number of rooms after** 18 **Number of apartments** 1 **Number of residents** 1 **Address** Chilterns, Oxfordshire, UK

18th century → 2011

For Park Corner Barn, a former cattle farm building has been transformed into a solid living environment.

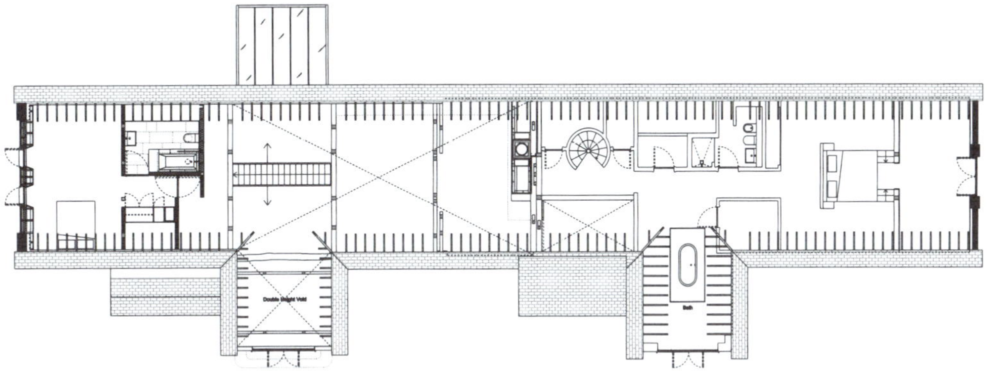

First floor plan

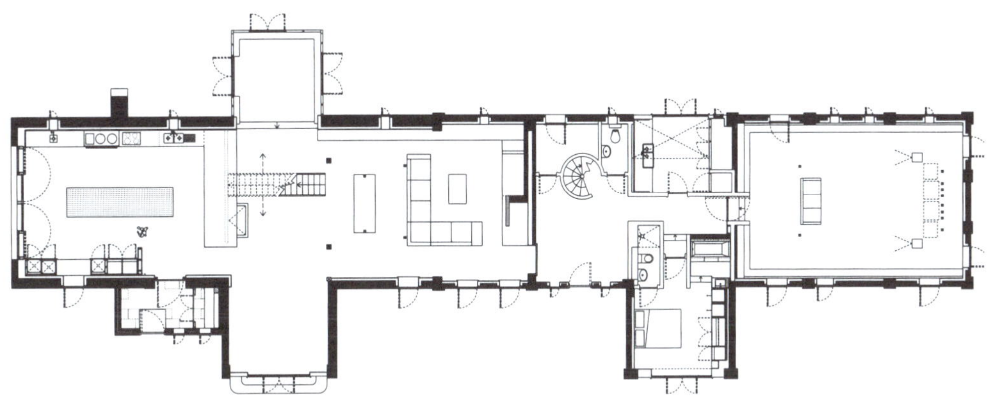

Ground floor plan

Two large living areas have been created where massive stone blocks and rough textures adapt the original interplay of brick and flint.

1950 → 2015

This former water storage facility now functions as a single-occupancy dwelling.

Building a single-occupancy home over a former water storage facility was the starting point of this project. The immediate environment has not been modified. The preexisting facility inspired the new design, with the curved glass façade following the lines of the former building. On the former paved platform, an object has emerged that overhangs the empty space, produced by the unevenness of the terrain. The lower level is sunken into the ground, creating a veranda that is placed outside the former platform. The upper floor of the house occupies the new prefabricated volume built with cross-laminated timber, sitting on top of a new metallic structure that does not interfere with the old structure. This volume shapes a big open space that functions simultaneously as living/dining room and kitchen, connecting the house with the garden.

A generous open-plan interior design offers a strong connection to the environment.

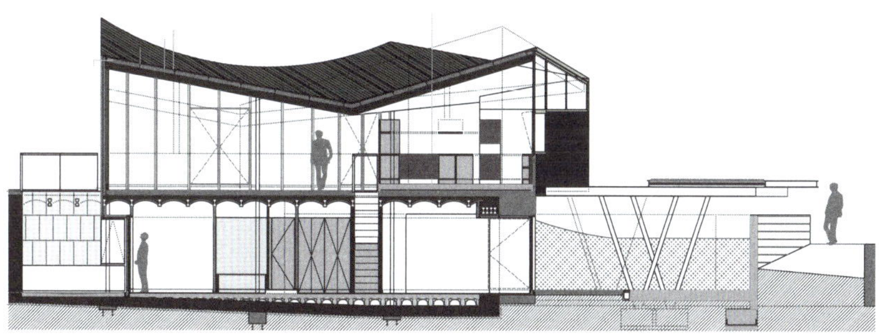

Section

Architect Alejandro Valdivieso (Valdivieso Arquitectos) **Completion** 2015 **Original building** Water cistern, 1950s **Gross floor area before** 75 m² **Gross floor area after** 170 m² **Number of rooms before** 1 **Number of rooms after** 3 **Number of apartments** 1 **Number of residents** 1 **Address** Calle Golondrinas 36B, 28430 Alpedrete, Madrid, Spain

The intervention carried out in the Conterie area involved transforming an industrial building into a residential building. Having lost its original function, the Conterie was a sort of enclosure in which the scale of the industrial complex, built between the 18th and 19th century, is in clear contrast with the minute urban scale of the island. The recovery program proposes a reintegration into the wider context of the entire island, and the introduction of new activities. The residential buildings have been built inside the existing factory. The dwellings on the façade are a "wall of rooms" leaning on the wall, while in the central part are the stairs and services alternated with openings in the volume; the living rooms face south, and the sequence of full and pierced walls, gardens and passages articulates the street between this building and the one facing it. Forming a sequence from public to private, the apartments repeat the tradition of Venetian urban structure.

19th century → 2015

Once an industrial space, the Conterie's Social Housing project now serves as a contemporary living environment in a dynamic setting.

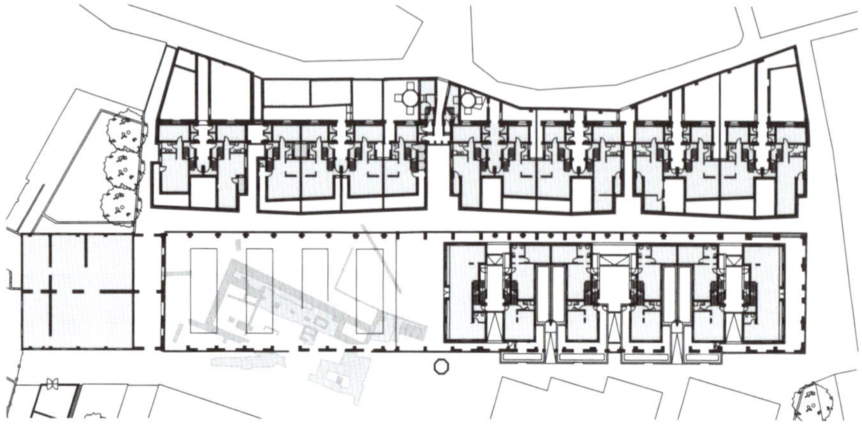

Ground floor plan after transformation

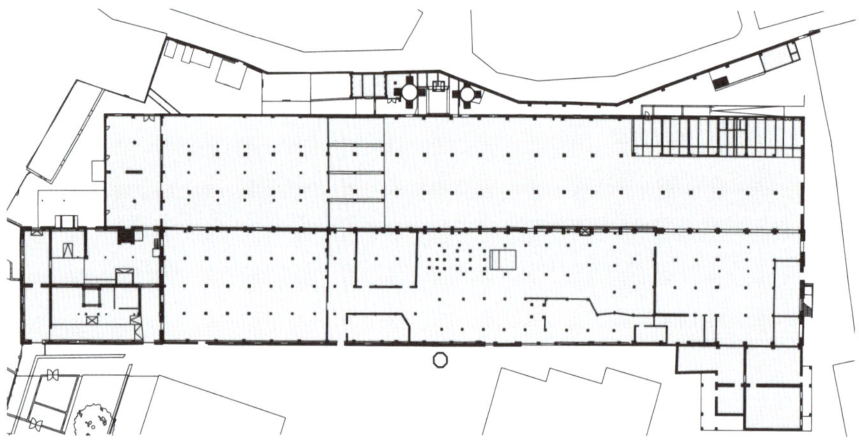

Ground floor plan before transformation

Architect Studio Macola **Completion** 2015 **Original building** Industrial building, 18th–19th century **Gross floor area before** 2,600 m² **Gross floor area after** 2,400 m² **Number of apartments** 36 **Number of residents** 108 **Address** Calle delle Conterie, Murano, Venice, Italy

The pragmatic character of this building has been preserved by integrating a sequence of space and various key elements.

The cheese warehouse "De Producent" in Gouda has undergone a spectacular transformation and now accommodates 52 residential lofts. A spacious atrium now forms the heart of the building. Because of the innovative reuse of elements from the old cheese warehouse, such as the original cheese boards, residents are still able to experience the 100-year-old history of making cheese. The existing floors have been used as a structural formwork for the new concrete floors, implemented in such a way that the original wooden ceilings remain visible and give the apartments a historic touch. Due to the strategic placement of loggias in the façade – maintaining the monumental rhythm of characteristic small windows – a diverse range of floor plans was possible. The residents are able to reach their apartment on one of the four floors through two glass elevators which go up and down along the historical façades.

1919/1949 → 2017

This former Gouda cheese warehouse has been turned into 52 luxury lofts.

Architect Mei architects and planners **Completion** 2017 **Original building** Cheese factory, 1919 and 1949 **Gross floor area** 5,000 m² **Number of apartments** 52 **Address** Westerkade 2, Gouda, the Netherlands

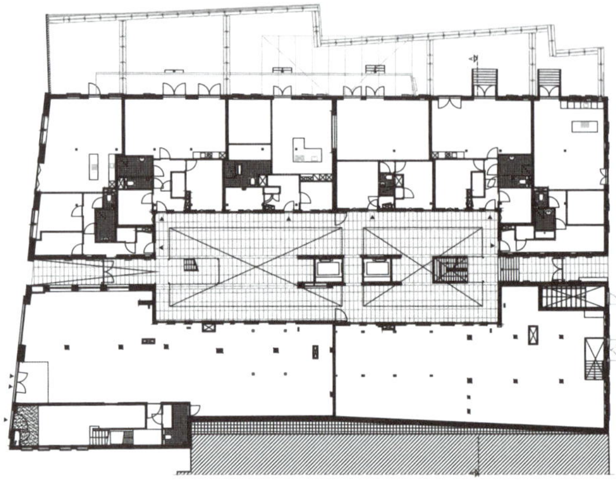

Ground floor plan

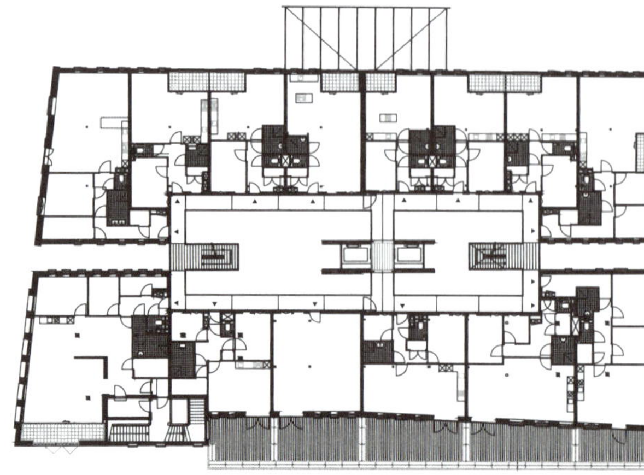

First floor plan

A mixture of preservation and reinterpretation led to a sophisticated design solution where old and new have been respected equally.

Once Europe's most modern granary, the 100-year-old Kattau-Mühle is a striking industrial monument and one of the most important buildings in the city of Buxtehude. Under consideration of guidelines regulating the preservation of historical buildings, this edifice has been renovated and altered where necessary. 14 apartments have been integrated into the upper stories of the former granary building. A single-story extension has been added at ground floor level, constructed as a light modern structure attached to the north side of the building. Each of the upper stories now houses four apartments and small steel balconies have been added where the former loading hatch was once located. The clever organization of the building elements has allowed the mill to remain a historic monument, despite its new role as a residential building.

1915 → 2015

Once an important grain silo, the Kattau-Mühle now houses 14 residences but has retained its role as industrial monument.

The addition of just a few building elements has supported the preservation of this monument with regional importance.

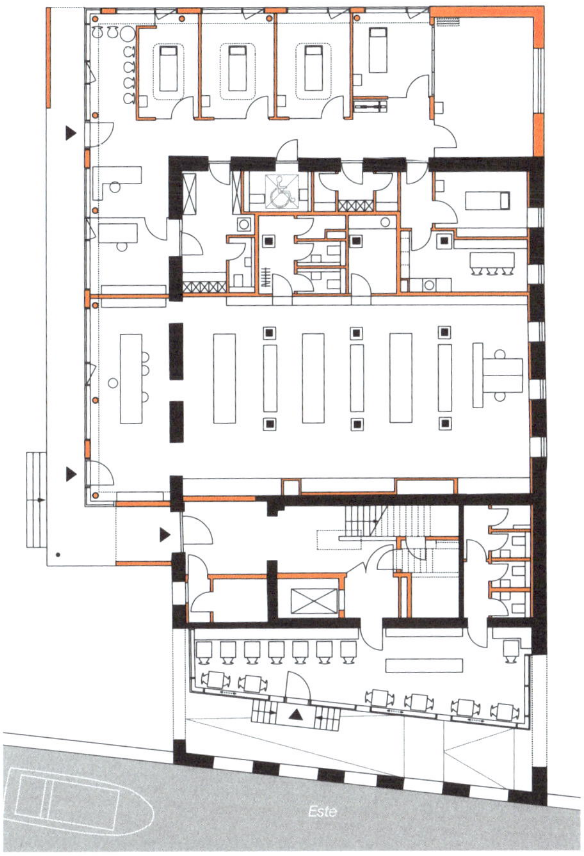

Ground floor plan

First floor plan

Architect KBNK Architekten **Completion** 2015 **Original building** Silo/ industrial complex by Martin Jank, 1915 **Gross floor area** 2,900 m^2 **Number of apartments** 14 **Address** Estebrügger Straße 2, 21614 Buxtehude, Germany

1967 → 2016

The Pacific impressively demonstrates how elegant a former dental school can be.

The Pacific is a new luxury condominium located in San Francisco's Pacific Heights neighborhood. The project included the adaptive reuse of a former 1960s dental school into a multifamily residential building, as well as the design of ten townhomes on an adjacent surface parking lot. The main building had essentially been built like a hospital, with high ceilings and large floor plates, which translated well to a luxury residential building: the floor plates, originally designed for heavy dental equipment, create high ceilings and gracious interior living spaces. The heavy precast concrete façade was replaced with a window wall system composed of champagne-colored metal panels and floor-to-ceiling glass. Window openings were made much larger, such that they are now the dominant feature in the façade. The townhouses were designed to relate in scale to the Victorian houses throughout the neighborhood. The exterior façades are composed of red cedar siding combined with silver metal panel and silvery glass that is lined in a brushed aluminum trim.

Architect Handel Architects **Completion** 2016 **Original building** Institutional building by Skidmore Owings and Merrill, 1967 **Gross floor area before** 20,800 m² **Gross floor area after** 21,900 m² **Number of apartments** 76 **Address** 2155 Webster Street, San Francisco, CA 94115, USA

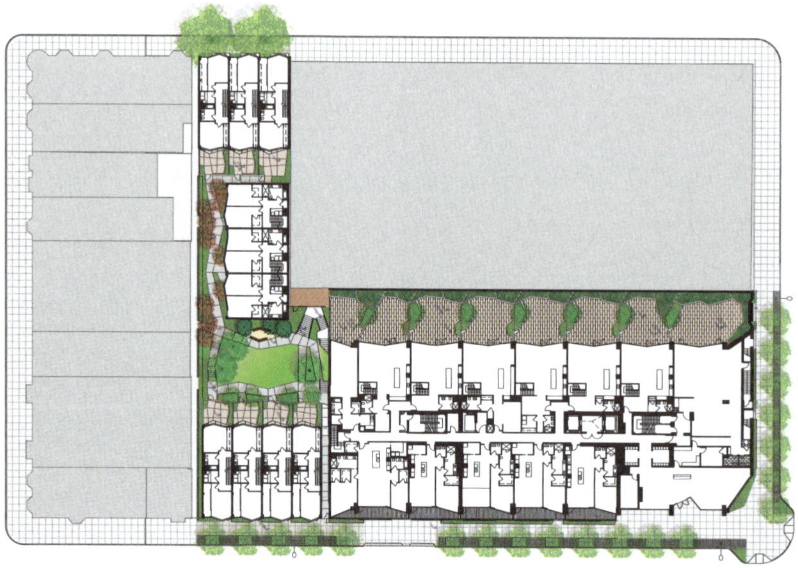

Ground floor plan

The preexisting high ceilings and large floor plates offered the perfect conditions for the establishment of a luxury multifamily complex.

1895 → 2016

The concept of Haus in Scheune uses a former barn as the architectural frame for a residential reinterpretation.

Located in a traditional village in Brandenburg, this unused barn has been utilized as the outer shell for a new residential property. From the outside, the barn has been left largely untouched, while a residential box has been added inside to create a "house in a house". This solution respects the historical character of the building, ensuring that the exterior appearance has been maintained so as not to disrupt the village esthetic. The new, transparent roof is the only element that signals the transformation. All of the exterior openings serve to provide direct and indirect lighting and ventilation. Inside the building, the closed, independent box solution has been placed on the existing concrete floor and the entire new space is conceived as an insulated timber construction. The interior walls comprise wooden boards, while plasterboard has been used to close the ceiling.

Architect RaumstarArchitekten **Completion** 2016 **Original building** Barn, 1895 **Gross floor area before** 120 m² **Gross floor area after** 85 m² **Number of rooms before** 1 **Number of rooms after** 2 **Number of apartments** 1 **Number of residents** 1 **Address** Treuenbrietzen, Germany

Establishing a house in house concept helped to maintain the traditional village ensemble, while connecting rural charm with functionality.

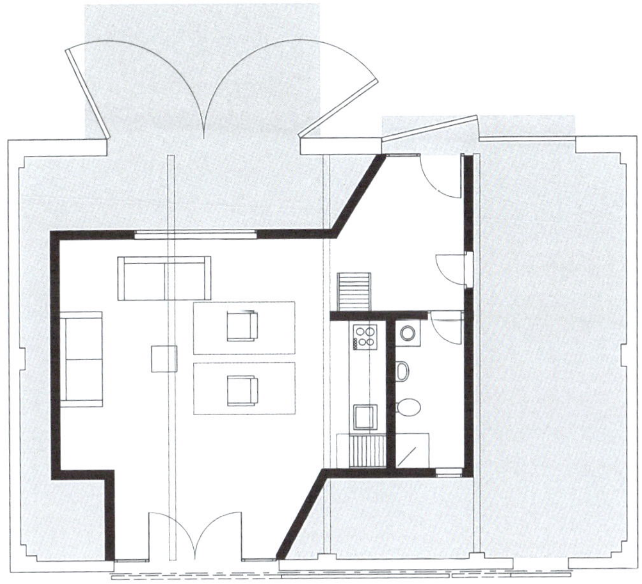

Ground floor plan: living area

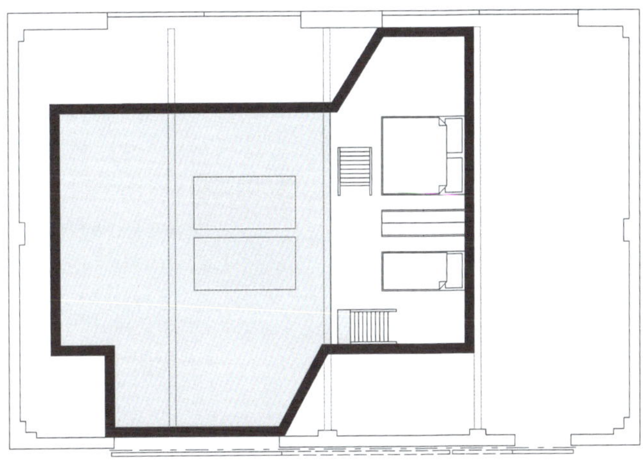

First floor plan: sleeping area

1910 → 2012

The Abbotsford Warehouse Apartments depict how industrial roughness can be turned into residential uniqueness.

This former industrial warehouse has been converted into two three-story warehouse apartments by removing the roof, retaining the lower floors and constructing a new upper floor which has been set back on all sides to create upper decks and balconies. Many of the old building's simple details were retained as well as the external walls and lower floors. New elements and materials sit side by side with the old to create contemporary apartments with old-world charm. Old timber workshop welding benches were retained and used for the kitchen island benches with new in-situ concrete bench tops added. New columns penetrate the island benches. Four-meter-high windows were converted into steel and glass front doors and electric garage doors to create an overwhelming effect upon entry, and match the scale of the existing four-meter-high ceilings. The old timber columns were removed, repaired and reinstated with concealed steel columns adjacent for strength.

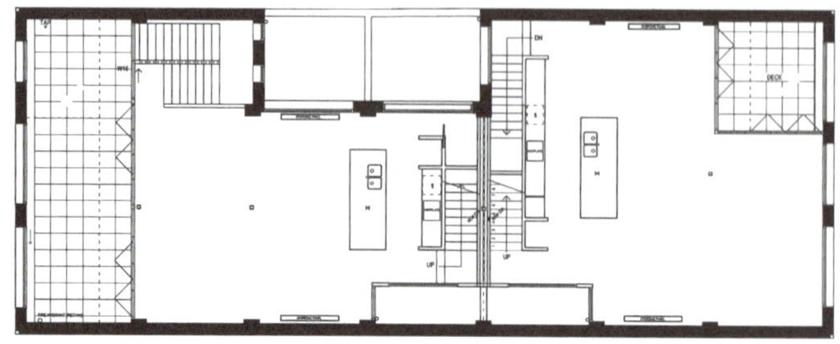

First floor plan

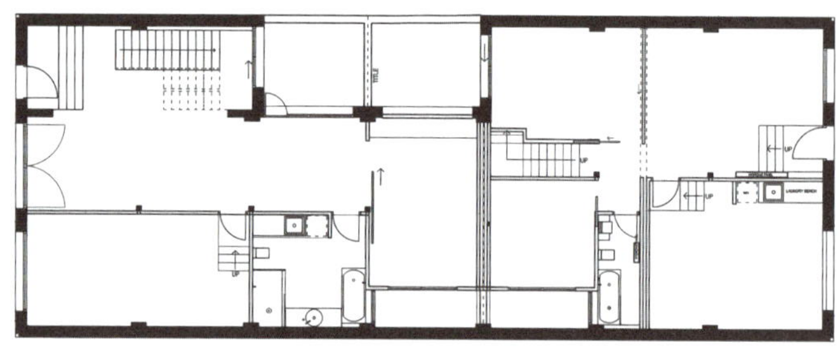

Ground floor plan

A sophisticated mixture of preservation and innovation led to a design that is determined by rustic details and old-world charm.

Architect ITN Architects **Completion** 2012 **Original building** Warehouse, 1910 **Gross floor area** 590 m^2 **Number of rooms before** 4 **Number of rooms after** 18 **Number of apartments** 2 **Number of residents** 4 **Address** 268 Langridge Street, Abbotsford, Victoria, Australia

Unknown → 2017

Once a commercial space, the project By Studio now serves as a contemporary living environment.

The focus of this project was the transformation of former commercial spaces into contemporary living spaces. Due to the nature of the original structures, the design of the new housing units is unconventional. The architects decided to create independent wooden structures that would simultaneously provide a solution for the spatial organization and also provide a functional structure for the residential units. The existing walls were covered with cabinets, thus providing storage space and ensuring acoustic and thermal comfort. The reorganization and reformulation of the preexisting sanitary facilities involved the construction of two colored modules. A yellow infrastructure contains the cooking area, while a blue serves other functions.

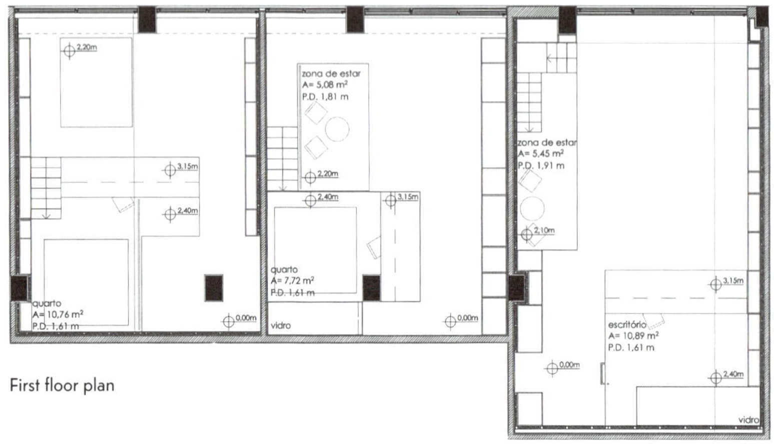

First floor plan

Ground floor plan

Architect WAATAA **Completion** 2017 **Original building** Commercial building **Gross floor area** 156.87 m² **Number of rooms** 2 per apartment **Number of apartments** 3 **Number of residents** 1 per apartment **Address** Telheiras, Lisbon, Portugal

The colored modules support the reorganization and provide a functional structure for the residential units.

Knevel Architecten was commissioned to transform a former office building, designed by W.M. Dudok, into student housing in Amsterdam. The approach taken respects the existing façade, renovating it where necessary. The student apartments were easily inserted into the existing structure of columns and concrete floors. Only some extra windows in the north and south façade were necessary to allow daylight to reach the rooms behind. For a better acoustic insulation from the adjacent highway, a double skin has been added to the west façade in the form of a loggia with a yellow frame. On the east façade, the yellow frame forms an internal windowsill. The characteristic canopy on the eleventh floor is emphasized with a graphic yellow print that from street level looks like autumn leaves. To level the connection between the student entrance on the east and the neighborhood, a raised public square has been added to the new entrance area.

1964 → 2015

Reusing the former Elsevier office building to create new student housing.

Yellow accents inside and outside the building carry connotations of positivity and clarity.

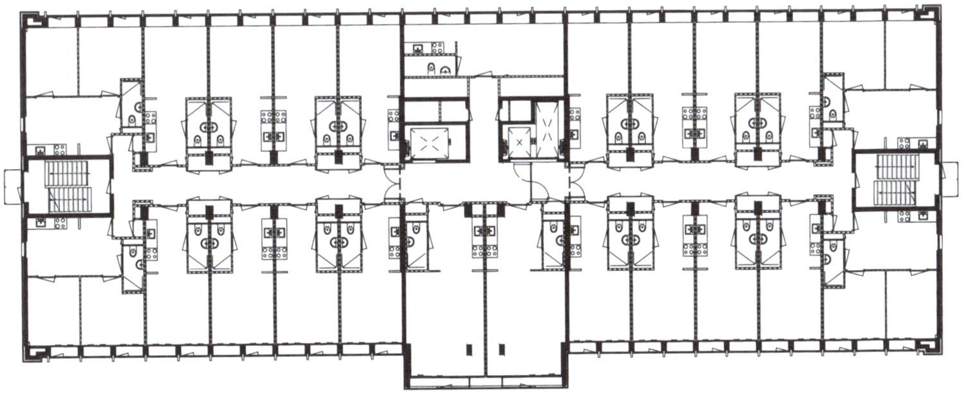

Floor plan

Architect Knevel Architecten **Completion** 2015 **Original building** Office, 1964 **Gross floor area** 11,750 m² **Number of rooms** 285 **Number of apartments** 285 **Number of residents** 285 **Address** Krelis Louwenstraat 5, Amsterdam, the Netherlands

1875 → 2017

With Pakhuis 't Glorie this former historical warehouse has been reused for pleasurable living.

This 19th-century warehouse is located close to the Royal Warehouse at Willemdock and was built shortly after the Antwerp ramparts were demolished by the merchant Jan Baptist Ceulemans. This warehouse is a valuable property because it is the only one remaining on Orange Street and most parts are still in their original condition or can be reconstructed easily. For example, the posts in the middle of the structure have been rebuilt to reintroduce the original rhythm of bays. From below, the timber of the floors is still visible on the ceilings, while seen from above it is hidden by underfloor heating. Sculp [IT] Architects have successfully remodeled this warehouse despite the tight budget. They preserved the building fabric and have added contemporary parts to ensure the building's suitability as a residential building and office.

Architect Sculp [IT] Architects **Completion** 2017 **Original building** Warehouse, 1875 **Gross floor area before** 400 m² **Gross floor area after** 350 m² **Number of apartments** 1 **Number of residents** 2 **Address** Antwerp, Belgium

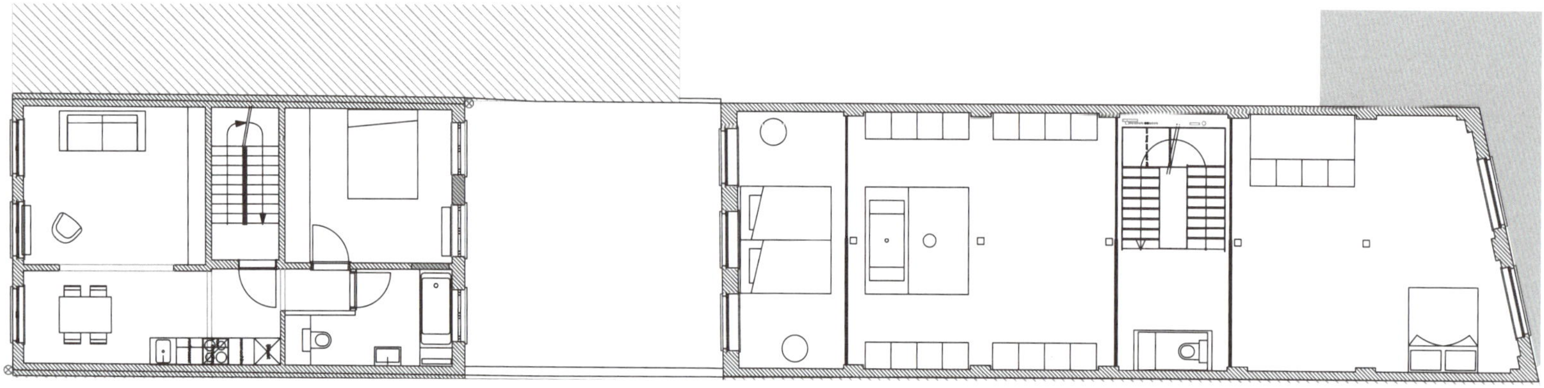

Floor plan

Parts of the original structure have been preserved, ensuring a warm and inviting atmosphere.

This warehouse from the early 20th century, with its sawtooth roof and brick walls overgrown with ivy, is like a green oasis in the city. The building has now been transformed into twelve residences. The lofts, organized back to back, each have their own entrance from the street. Where once the loading and unloading doors stood, are now large sliding gates made of perforated steel. The pattern of holes is inspired by old photographs of the factory interior; a different image is used for each gate. Behind these fences are sheltered loggias, which act as private front gardens where bicycles can be kept, and where the front doors are located. The design has a clear dichotomy. The entrance, WC, and technical functions are bundled in one zone, with the bedrooms and a roof terrace on the first floor. The rest of the space remains looking like a factory, the steel trusses remain visible and have simply been brushed clean.

1920 → 2015

This former gearwheel factory in Amsterdam now houses 12 extraordinary lofts.

Architect Ronald Janssen Architecten **Completion** 2015 **Original building** Gearwheel factory, 1920 **Gross floor area before** 1,180m^2 **Gross floor area after** 1,680 m^2 **Number of apartments** 12 **Number of residents** Approx. 42 **Address** Nieuwe Ridderstraat 43–53 & Nieuwe Jonkerstraat 50–60, Amsterdam, the Netherlands

Ground floor plan

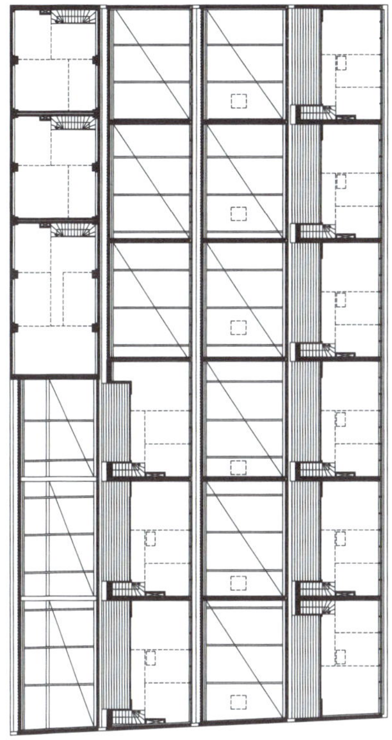

First floor plan

New zones function as pragmatic areas for the residences, while the main character maintains the open structure typical of a factory.

1932 → 2014

Docks Malraux revived this former industrial building in the port of Strasbourg for new living space.

The old Seegmuller warehouse is part of a huge and remarkable industrial ensemble located in Strasbourg's port area: La Presqu'île Malraux. The longitudinal island of this 600-meter-long artificial dock is composed of a 50-meter central tower and two low-rise buildings. Right from the very beginning, the architects wished to preserve the industrial patrimony. The initial use of the existing building, with its strong reinforced concrete permitted the replacement of the old tile roof with a metallic three-story superstructure. Steel was chosen due to its lightness and esthetics. The metal exoskeleton, inspired by the port's rhetoric, reinterprets the grid and features of the existing building. In an almost Mies-like sobriety and refinement, the new part has skin of glass and bones of steel. The 15-meter huge cantilever on the western façade shelters the central piazza.

Architect Cabinet d'Architecture et d'Urbanisme Georges HEINTZ & associés **Completion** 2014 **Original building** Warehouse, 1932 **Gross floor area before** 7,000 m² **Gross floor area after** 11,600 m² **Number of apartments** 67 **Address** Presqu'île Malraux, 67000 Strasbourg, France

ARMEMENT SEEGMULLER
RESTAURANT
LEON DE
BRUXELLES
PUB & BRASSERIE
AU BUREAU
PUB & BRASSERIE

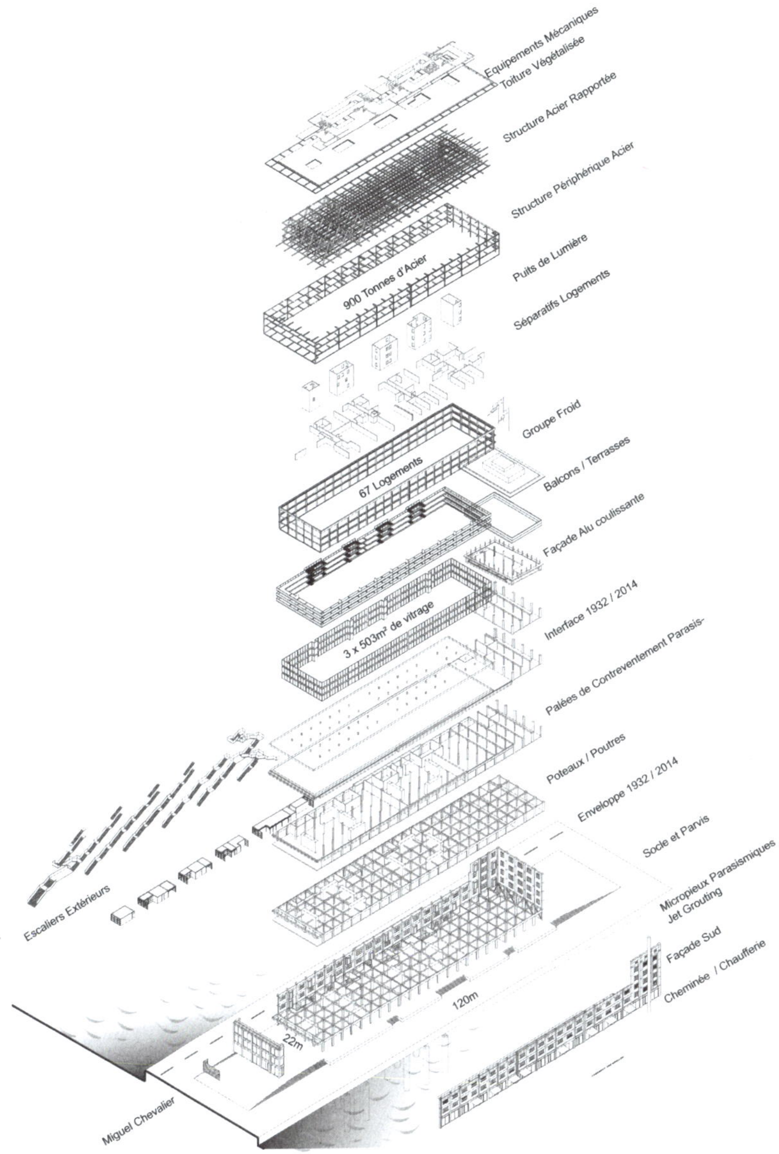

Axonometry

The metallic exoskeleton returns to the port's rhetoric and gives the building a filigree character and solidity at the same time.

This project consists essentially of the transformation of a warehouse and distribution center from the 1950s. The main task was to develop 18 apartments, rescuing as many of the original features as possible in order to remain within the tight budget. The basic idea was to create a framework for the new housing program by reinforcing and taking advantage of the existing structure. The main challenge was to provide uniformity and standardize the façade elements, which previously comprised a combination of different styles. Simple elements and strong, inexpensive materials have been used, resulting in a striking architectural design. An Irving mesh has been used to provide a more unified esthetic, allow sunlight to seep through and to address security concerns. This additional skin gives the building a sober, simple and elegant look.

Architect Archetonic **Completion** 2012 **Original building** Warehouse, 1950s **Gross floor area after** 1,883 m² **Number of rooms before** 1 **Number of rooms after** 23 **Number of apartments** 18 **Number of residents** 18 families **Address** Comercio 117, Del. Miguel Hidalgo, Mexico City, Mexico

1950s → 2012

For Comercio 117, a former warehouse has been transformed into 18 apartments.

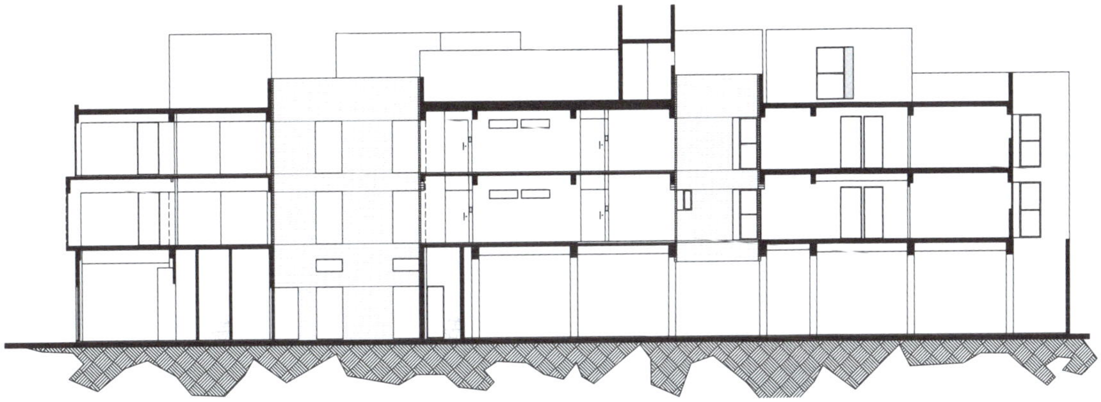

Longitudinal section

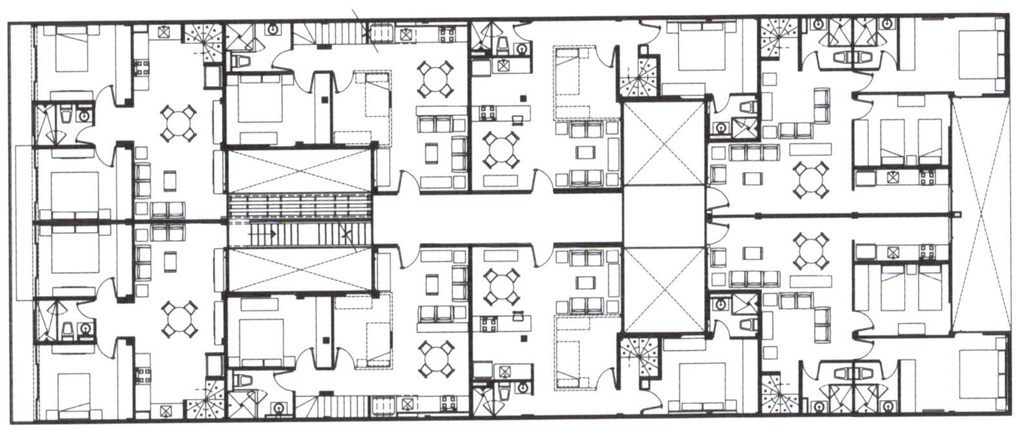

First floor plan

A new façade and reorganization of the inner structures guarantee a consistent impression.

Unknown → 2017

Warehouse HM expressively demonstrates that industrial design and a welcoming ambience must not exclude each other.

Designed for a multitalented animal-loving couple, whose hobbies include hosting, painting and baking workshops, this abode offers the dwellers plenty of space for their activities as well as roaming space for their five pets. The property was previously a warehouse. The clients asked design collective Lim + Lu to maintain the rawness of the space while transforming it into a family home and creative workshop that can house the couple's existing furniture and memorabilia. The area has been divided into two halves – private and public. Upon entering through a decrepit factory door that has been left in its original condition, visitors are greeted by a minimal vestibule containing only a bench and a shoe cabinet. Peeling back the adjacent industrial sliding door will reveal a painting workshop populated with supplies. Peeling back a second sliding door exposes the spacious and light-filled living space.

LET'S

weddings

Architect Lim + Lu **Completion** 2017 **Original building** Warehouse **Gross floor area** 242 m² **Number of rooms before** 1 **Number of rooms after** 7 **Number of apartments** 1 **Number of residents** 2 **Address** Hong Kong, China

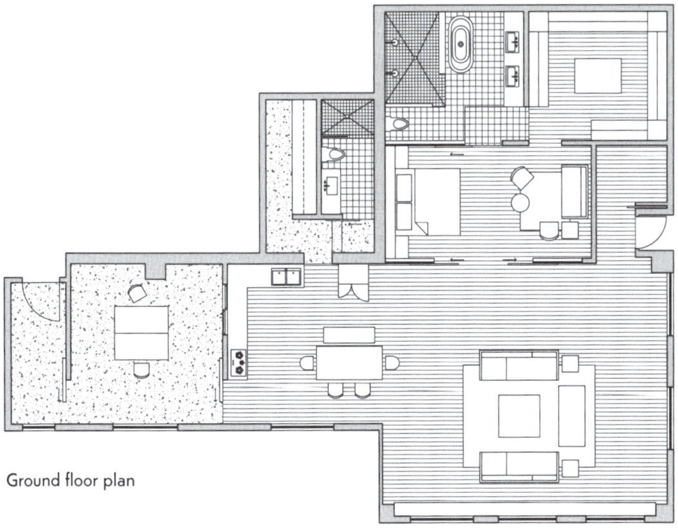

Ground floor plan

Sliding doors help to divide the space into different zones, thus taking advantage of the former open-plan structure without losing a sense of privacy.

1974 → 2017

The former office complex at Frankfurter Tor now houses serviced apartments and student accommodation.

Reinforced concrete columns along the exterior walls and inside this former office building, together with the reinforced concrete ceilings, provide a solid supporting structure. The building has been completely renovated and a new story was added. The color scheme used for the façade references the copper roofs of the towers at Frankfurter Tor. The complex now houses a total of 567 residential units, 485 of which are student apartments, and 82 micro-apartments grouped around an attractive inner courtyard. Large landscaped areas offer space for residents to relax and function as popular communal spaces. The large student lobby functions as a central attraction and offers ideal conditions for flexible use. The student apartments range from 18 to 24 square meters in size, while the serviced apartments are between 25 and 39 square meters.

Architect GBP Architekten **Completion** 2017 **Original building** Office complex, approx. 1974 **Gross floor area before** 13,553 m² **Gross floor area after** 25,711 m² **Number of apartments** 567 **Address** Frankfurter Tor 8A / Warschauer Straße 5–8, 10243 Berlin, Germany

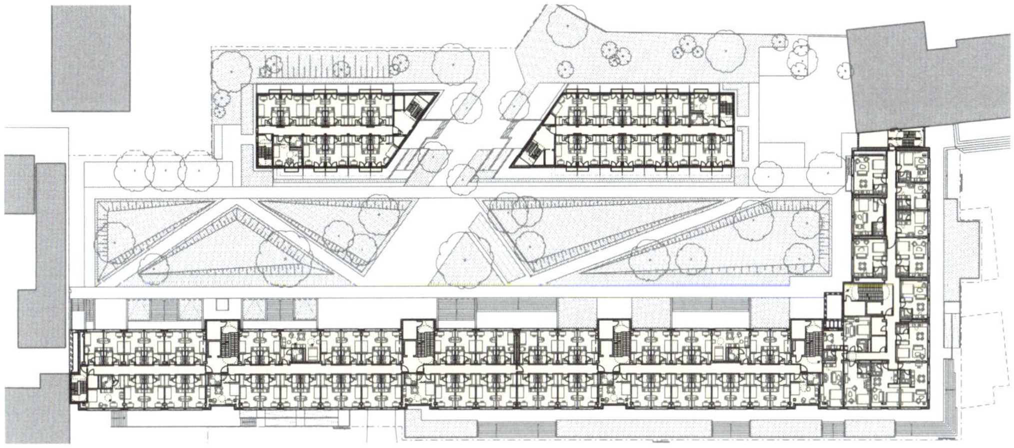

Standard floor plan

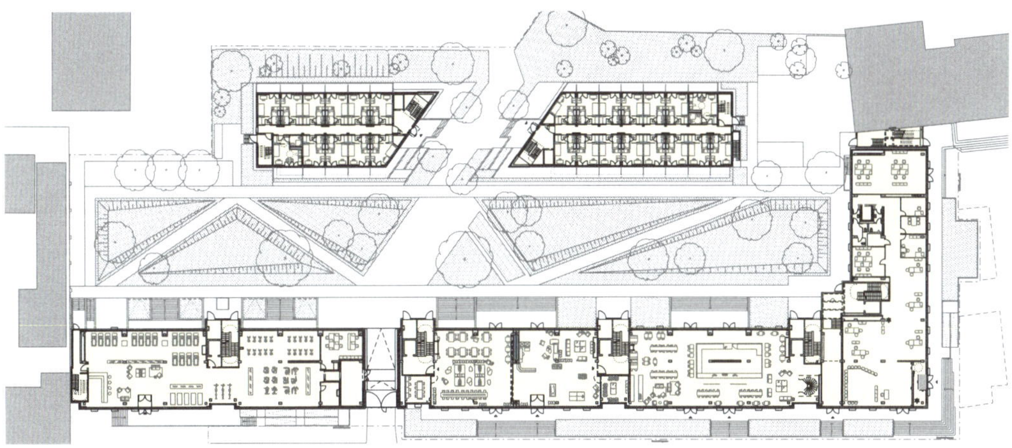

Ground floor plan

The reinforced concrete skeleton has been preserved and now houses vibrant community spaces and residences.

1932 → 2016

Paraden brought a former cinema back to life as a luxury living space with distinctive 1930s charm.

Paraden, one of Stockholm's earliest functionalist cinemas, has been converted into luxury flats with an adjoining restaurant. The biggest challenge was to preserve the characteristic functionalist elements while allowing the restrained, well-balanced design to be reflected in surfaces and fittings in the new flats as well as in the ground floor restaurant. According to Andreas Martin-Löf the preconditions for this type of development were excellent thanks to the layout of the original building. Interesting features inside the flats include column walls and a span ceiling. The narrow fenestration allows for compact interior spaces with plenty of natural light. Each flat faces a light well where residents are able to cultivate their own gardens. Monica Förster Design Studio was responsible for the tailor-made interior design, kitchens, bathroom cabinets, wardrobes and fittings. The chosen colors and materials reflect those of the former cinema.

The colors and materials recall the atmosphere of the former cinema, thus melting timeless elegance and Scandinavian lifestyle.

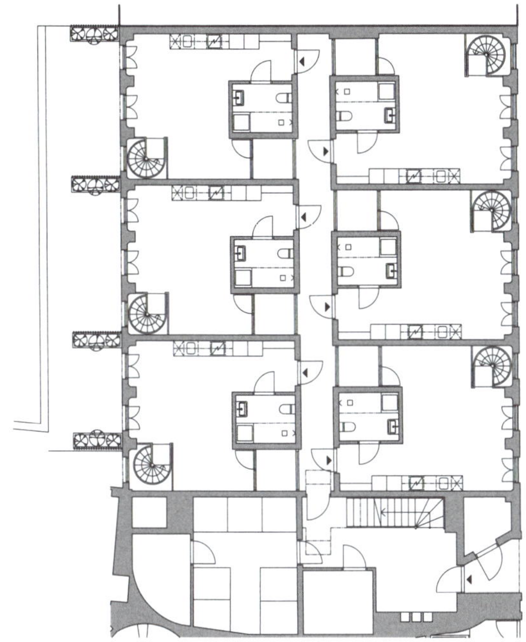

Ground floor plan whole structure

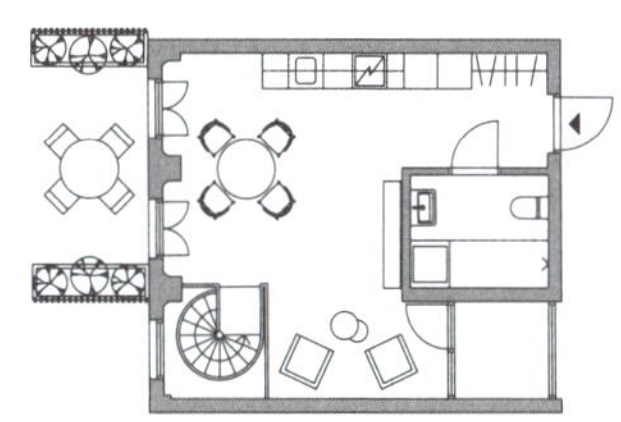

Ground floor plan apartment one

Architect Andreas Martin-Löf **Completion** 2016 **Original building** Cinema by Björn Hedvall, 1932 **Gross floor area apartments** 35–85 m² **Number of apartments** 12 **Number of residents** 16 **Address** Östermalm, Stockholm, Sweden

1903 → 2016

With the Residences at PS 186 a former public school has been turned into a vivid space of communal and socio-cultural importance.

This former five-story school has been converted into a mixed-use development, offering the community vital affordable housing and a new home for the Boys and Girls Club of Harlem. The design approach is informed by a deep respect for the building's architectural past. The façade, cornice, window units, and glass doors were recreated from historic photographs and drawings of the original building. The original cornice was recreated true to proportion, size, and detail. Based on remaining materials, the courtyards' decorative metal railings and gates were reconstructed as well as the existing stone stairs. Working within the original H-ground floor plan of the school, former classrooms were transformed into a robust mix of apartment unit layouts for low to moderate income households.

Architect Dattner Architects **Completion** 2016 **Original building** Public school, 1903 by C.B.J. Snyder **Gross floor area** 10,405 m² **Number of apartments** 79 **Address** 526 W 146th St, New York, NY 10031, USA

PUBLIC SCHOOL

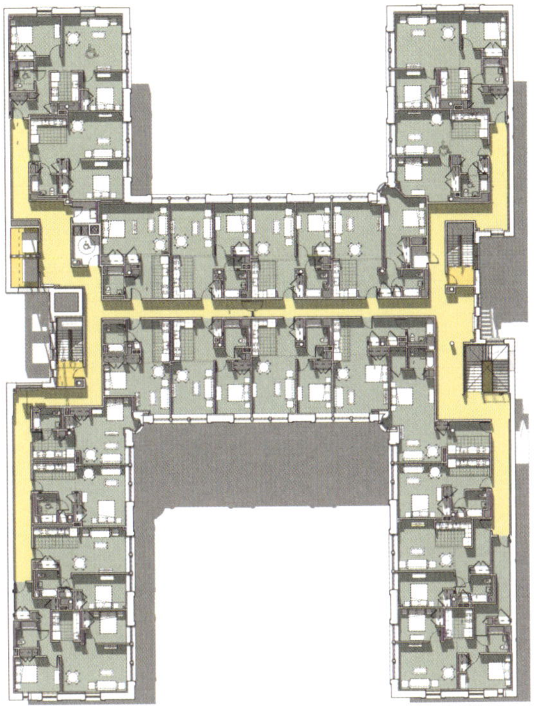

Third floor plan

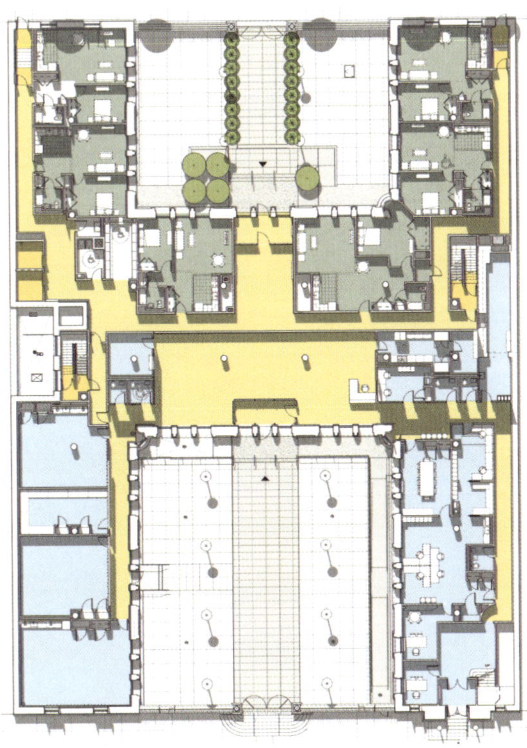

Ground floor plan

Additional character-defining details were preserved such as the interior track hallway, and classroom corridor transoms.

Index

Picture credits

100% interior Sylvia Leydecker / Photographer: Reinhard Rosendahl 62–65
Arthur Bagen 30, 31 a., b., 32 a., 33
Gabriele Basilico / Milan 202 r.
Nirut Benjabanpot 252–257
BM. / flickr.com CC0 7 b.
Boureau David 110 b., 112 a., 113 a. r.
Andreas Buchberger 162–165
Youri Claessens / www.youriclaessens.com 34–39
Diego Cosme 118–123
Lucia Crista 60–61
Arno de la Chapelle / Oulu 178–183
René de Wit / Breda 12–15
Johan Dehlin / Stockholm 102–104
destilat 26–29
Andreas Diglas / Gockhausen 106–109
Dorfmüller / Klier 212–215
Lyndon Douglas / London 152–155
Leonard Fäustle 232–235
Germain Ferey 130–133
David Frutos / BIS Images 198–201
Zaiga Gaile 125 b.
Rafael Gamo 248–251
Martin Gardner 54–57
Adriá Goula 48–53
Anton Grassl 117
Gross & Daley 188–193
Scott Hargis Photo / San Francisco 216, 217 a. l., b., 218, 219 a. l., r.
Jörg Hempel 156–161
Lionel Henriod 166–169
Anastasia Hermann / Berlin 258–261
Hildegard Hick 31 c., 32 b.
Chris Humphreys 20–25
Hertha Hurnhaus 88–93
Industryous Photography 184–187
Miran Kambič u.d.i.a. 76–79
Jonathan Kannair 114
Julia Klug / www.juliaklug.com 80–83
Luuk Kramer / Amsterdam 240–243
Angela Lamprecht 134–137
Peter Landers / London 138–141
Langridge Street photos / Michael Downes 225 b., 226
Åke E:son Lindman 262–265
Babis Loizidis / Athens 146–151
Ainas Meiers 127 b., 128 a. l.
Udo Meinel 220–223
Mireca / flickr.com CC BY 2.0 6–7
Mollison Street photos / Mathew Moore 224, 225 a. r., 227 a., b.
Cornelius Morscher 85 b. l.
Ollynet68 / flickr.com CC BY-ND 2.0 7 a.
Mikael Olsson / Stockholm 105
Youngchae Park 98–101
Marcin Andrzej Pawlowski / Paris 94–97
Michael Pfisterer / Hamburg 44–47
Robert Pfurtscheller 67 b.
Florian Pipo / Munich 170–173
Jesper Ray 70–75
Wolfgang Retter / Lienz 66, 67 a., 68–69
Luc Roymans 236–239
Philippe Ruault / Paris 244–246
Cesar Rubio / San Francisco 219 b. l.
Douglas Shoop 115 l., b. r., 116 a., b.
Jakub Skokan / BoysPlay Nice 40–43
Ansis Starks 124, 125 a., 126 l., 127 a., 128 a. r., 129
David Sundberg / Esto / New York 266–269
Hannah Taylor 194–197
Dominique Uldry / Berne 84, 85 a., b. r., 86–87
Ossip van Duivenbode 206–211
Albert Vecerka / Esto / New York 8–11
Christophe Voisin 16–19
Waataa Photography! 228–231
Matthew Williams / NYC 142–145
Marco Zanta / Treviso / Italy 202 l., 203, 204–205
Yohan Zerdoun 174–177
Antonin Ziegler 110, 111, 112 b., 113 a. l.

All other pictures were made available by the architects and designers.

Cover front: Julia Klug/www.juliaklug.com
Cover back: Jakub Skokan / BoysPlay Nice, Adriá Goula, Martin Gardner (from left to right, from above to below)